A Soldier Like Jack

Jack

Based on a true story

Perhaps Jack and your
father-in-law knew one
another? I think Jack
would have been drawn to
the mules, as everyone in my
family has loved animals.
...you never know!

Clare Cogbill

All good wishes to you

Julie

(Clare :-)

Clare Cogbill

A Soldier Like Jack
Clare Cogbill has asserted her right under the Copyright,
Designs and Patents Act 1988 to be identified
as the author of this work.

This book is sold subject to the condition that it
shall not, by way of trade or otherwise, be lent,
resold, hired out, or otherwise circulated without
the author's prior consent.

This book is the author's
personal expression of events as researched by her and
supported by family archive evidence.
Some peripheral characters are fictional, however all the
family members are real and do/did exist. Events, names
or places have been changed where requested and as
necessary to protect the identity of those individuals.

The author accepts no responsibility for how
others may interpret her work.
First published in 2014

ISBN-13: 978-1500701369 (CreateSpace-Assigned)
ISBN-10: 150070136X

There was a place

Where the branches swayed gently in the
breeze

Casting amber gold leaves

That swirled to the ground

And children danced and laughed and sang

Oblivious to the turmoil in their land

(Clare Cogbill)

In Memory of

The Holmes and Cogbill families of the early to mid-1900s

especially

Jack Cogbill and Grace Cogbill (previously Holmes)

&

George Cogbill and Agnes Cogbill (previously Jelfs)

...and for Mum (1939 – 2014) and Dad (1936 – 1971) who are together once more

ACKNOWLEDGMENTS

It is difficult with a book such as this to know when to stop, to know when you've written enough – when does the story become whole? When have you said all that's to be said? There is an almost insatiable desire to keep on digging and digging for information, but eventually I realised that this is just one family of the millions of families around the world whose ancestors were affected by the war and, there is a limit, so I have to let the story go – just let it be what it is.

My dear mum, Maureen, who died before she got the chance to read this in its final form. You were the one for whom I was writing it, and it feels strange that you're not here to share in the end-product. I shall miss your wise words for as long as I live.

For helping me through the loss of Mum and supporting me through the final stages of this book, you've all been brilliant – so a huge thank you to Alun R. McMorran and Connor A. McMorran – you two, and our three dogs, are my world (and Connor, thank you for yet another wonderful book cover). You are both amazing. Mark Smith – for the history and especially for pointing out that part which the rest of us had missed. Pat Smith – for being a huge part of telling me the story – you were *actually* a part of Grace's world. Fred Holmes – I've never met you, but your story has helped me very much with this.

Rose Conway for your India feedback and for our many years of friendship. My friends, Pat Pickering – once again your attention to detail is impeccable, Steve for your historical information, Elaine Olney, for the 'feelings' and the 'flow', Jan McMorran – for reading this on your way to Brittany, Will Rutherford – for the history (Tanya, you can read the next one for me), and Sheena Traills – thank you. Also a huge thank you to all at Dumfries Writers' Group.

To the authors of the texts I used to expand my knowledge of The Great War, I am hugely grateful – these gave me a foundation on which to build the Cogbill story. There exists particularly useful regimental records for both the Warwickshire and the Worcester regiments. These provided me with a fascinating insight into chronological events for George and Edwin's battalions. Many of Jack's war records survived the fires which destroyed so many WW1 records, and this information was invaluable.

The world is very different now, and there is a sense that we would never allow atrocities such as those which occurred in WW1 to happen again, but in the news we see the same images of war time and time again. We, the human race, need to constantly remind ourselves of the sacrifices that were made by our ancestors and learn what we should have learned a century ago.

Grace Cogbill 1912

Prologue

1956

Her hands shaking and knotted with tiresome age, Grace carefully placed her cup and saucer back on the table. Despite her best intentions, the saucer still rattled: bone china against bone china; bone china against wood.

Maureen was in the kitchen making a cup of tea for herself, her brother Bobby, and sister Pattie. She shouted through to see whether her grandmother wanted another cup, but Grace declined; the one in front of her she had secretly added a shot of rum to before her grandchildren arrived.

Holding her tea in front of her with both hands, and with the steam from her cup now warming her face, Maureen sat opposite her grandmother, and between her brother and sister. They patiently waited for the rasping of Grace's lungs to subside so they could hear from her why she had called them all together. Tommy, Grace's scruffy old tan and white terrier-type dog, raised his head from where he had nestled down next to Maureen's feet, checking for any morsels which might be coming his way.

Once Grace's breathing had settled into an acceptable rhythm, she reached forward for the small, battered, green tin she had carefully positioned next to her cup.

She eased off the lid and reached inside for a pinch of brown, withered tobacco leaves and began to crumble them along the length of the white strip of paper. She contemplated the fresh, young faces of the three teenagers in front of her: Maureen – eighteen now and courting a young man named Tony; Bobby – sixteen and been working for two years now; sweet young Pattie – still just a girl but looking forward to the day when she would be able to leave school. It wouldn't be long now. As she licked the edge of the cigarette paper, Grace hesitated and wondered whether Pattie was perhaps a little too young for what she had to show them today.

A shadow of concern cast itself across Maureen's face as she watched her grandmother rolling the cigarette, and Grace smiled at her, momentarily revealing the gaps between her yellowed teeth; Maureen had long ago stopped discouraging her grandmother from smoking – although just last week there had been reports on the wireless about how smoking could give you cancer. It was too late for Grace – she was dying, and in the last few weeks Maureen in particular had noticed a peaceful acceptance enveloping her grandmother like a warm blanket. This woman who had nurtured them since they were born knew that if she didn't do this now, then all she had known, all she had loved, would be laid to rest with her in the grave on the hill. *'What use was there in knowing a story but only telling half of it?'* Grace thought.

Maureen, Bobby and Pattie had never tired of hearing about Jack and the old days, and through all the preceding years Grace had left out the parts she knew her grandchildren would find disturbing, keeping the finer details bottled up deep inside her. The laughter lines of her youth disguised now in the creases that had become the map of her face, Grace's eyes sparkled as they had done when she had married Jack back in 1912. In her hands was a large, black book with the words 'Back Then: Jack and Me – by Grace Cogbill' written across the front. She passed it across the table to the three eager young people and said 'I wrote this for you, it's the whole story.' She settled back in the chair, relaxing as she pursed her lips over the end of her cigarette, the end of it glowing as she inhaled the smoke deeply; deeper and deeper the smoke travelled, carrying the nicotine which coated her throat and silently crept its way down into the depths of her lungs.

Maureen took the book from her and carefully turned its pages to reveal her grandmother's familiar handwriting, a clear script which was interspersed with photographs and mementoes such as old, faded postcards. Flicking back to the start, she began to read the words aloud to her younger brother and sister.

Once her cigarette was finished, Grace rested her head on the wing of the armchair and listened closely to the story for which she had painstakingly gathered documents and photographs over the preceding few years.

After casting his eyes towards the edge of a plate of sweet-smelling biscuits he couldn't quite reach, Tommy admitted defeat and lay down on the rug. He let out a long, deep sigh and rested his head across Maureen's stockinged feet.

It was going to be a long day.

Chapter 1

Back in 1912

Jack.

Yes, I imagine that's where we should start, because I suppose everything that has happened since then has revolved around him.

When Jack informed me that he wanted to go and talk to my father about something 'important', my heart felt as though it would burst with excitement. Standing outside my house with a look of dread etched on his face while he waited for an eruption of courage to lead him into the dragon's lair, I kissed him on the cheek and told him I was going down the road to find my sister Florrie.

It wasn't that my father was a frightening man, although I imagine to a man of small stature with such a gentle nature as Jack had, he could be quite terrifying. My father was tall and big, not fat, but very muscular, you see, and he was a military man who had worked in India and Africa – he had been a sergeant in the Boer War, working as a gunsmith; I suppose when it came to it, Jack was quite daunted at the prospect of asking him if he could marry his daughter.

While Jack paced up and down in our front garden, perhaps subconsciously wanting to impress my father with his marching skills, I left him pondering his approach while I raced to the grocery shop to tell Florrie my news. Darting into the shop and nearly knocking over a display of canned foods, I screeched with excitement as I told Florrie that Jack had asked me to marry him – well, not exactly, but I knew that was what he wanted to speak to Father about.

Florrie threw her arms around my neck and, after she turned and shouted to Mrs. Brown that she'd be back in ten minutes, we made our way to the house where we saw the front door close just as we reached the end of the garden.

Sneaking to the front window, we looked around the edge of the curtain and saw the familiar scene of Father sitting with the side of his head in view, a newspaper on his lap and a cigar protruding from his moustached mouth. He had one of those moustaches that filled the space between his mouth and nose and which curled up at its edges. He was very proud of his bushy, grey moustache, and would sit pulling the hairs out straight, letting them ping back into position whenever he was considering something. We watched as, up went his hand, and out came the edge of his moustache. I had never found it endearing before, but that day I did. Jack stood awkwardly next to my father's armchair and he looked terrified. I am sure it was no surprise to my parents that Jack and I would want to marry, but that didn't stop Father's military background from allowing him to revel just a little in the poor boy's embarrassment.

Outside, Florrie and I huddled together, giggling at Jack's predicament until, finally, he nodded and shook hands with Father. I couldn't help noticing Jack's face was flushed scarlet to the tips of his prominent ears; I had never noticed them protruding like that before, but it just made me love him more.

As he emerged through the front door, Jack's face broke into the widest of smiles. Rushing over to me, he grasped me around the waist and spun me around and around in the middle of the street. Feeling dizzy once he'd stopped spinning me, I noticed Florrie was now stood in the doorway flanked by our parents, my father with his cigar still glowing under his moustache. Was that the flicker of a smile I could see which was being masked by the cigar? I have always wondered that and I would like to think that it was.

We set the date for later that year – a romantic Christmas Eve wedding. We couldn't wait for the time to come when we would be married and could start a family. Jack was working making chocolates for the local factory in Bournville, and I was working on the presses for a local metal works. I would have to give up my job when we got married. But, strangely, I didn't mind – it was what most of we women did.

When I first met Jack he was fascinated that I had been born in Sitapur, in India – I suppose it was somewhere he had previously known nothing about. He had hardly ever been out of the Midlands except for a couple of trips to Weston-Super-Mare when he was a boy. He was disappointed that I couldn't really remember anything about it. Each time he asked me about what I did remember about India he became increasingly fascinated and pleaded with me to try to remember more, but I was just a small girl when we left there, and so anything I *could* remember was vague and disjointed. The uniforms of the men Father worked with were meshed in my mind with the bright colours of the streets and marketplaces with their heaps of fragrant spices at every stall, and the silk, satin, and sequinned clothes of the people who worked there. The heat was sometimes unbearable, and I told Jack about how I could remember the rays from the sun that used to sear our fair skin, burning the layers until we came out in painful blisters.

Jack said he wanted to travel one day – he wanted to take me to exotic places to see those bright colours again, and eat food which could only grow in such a climate. I could remember large boats and expansive oceans – Father took us everywhere he went and we lived in army accommodation. It was exciting, but we never felt settled. I suppose we were always anticipating the next move and that stopped us from laying down roots. We went on a ship to South Africa in 1905. I remember that it was called the SS Bramer Castle. I don't know why I remember that, it seems such a strange thing to recall after everything that has happened.

The fact that I remembered so little from those days back in India didn't matter to Jack when he talked about me to his brothers George, Henry, Alfred, Edwin and Frank. I was the special one, the glamorous girl who had been born in a faraway land, the one who had sipped exotic juices and who had bathed in foreign seas. Not that his brothers were particularly interested though – George had Agnes and his two daughters, Aggie and Frances; Henry spent all his time with his head in the clouds talking about leaving England and going to live in America; Alfred was the quiet one and you never quite knew what he was thinking; Edwin was just becoming a man; and little Frank was just a small child who followed their only sister, Beck, around as though he thought she would run away and leave him. Their mother, Mary-Ann, had her hands full, but she coped well, and each one of her offspring had turned out just fine. They were not a well-off family, and I had worried about that when Father found out Jack and I were sweet on one another, but he accepted the situation better than I thought he would.

George and Agnes married six years before we did. Agnes was lovely – a calm, solid type with dark brown hair which she pulled back from her face into a bun at the nape of her neck. She had serious, deep brown eyes which at times made her look fierce, but when she smiled, laughter lines creased their corners. She and George had known each other for almost the whole of their lives, but to Jack that was boring. Childhood sweethearts they may have been, but Jack thought India was something else.

Jack and his family came from a little village in the Cotswolds – Long Compton. He took me there once when we were courting. We took a picnic and left really early to go and catch the train. When I saw this beautiful place where he had been born, I couldn't help but be fascinated by the 'Englishness' of the buildings. There were limestone houses with limestone walls enclosing the gardens and, just peeking over the tops of the walls were fragrant honeysuckles, creeping jasmine, and luscious fruit trees. It was positively the most beautiful place I had ever been. I may have travelled the world when I was a young girl, but Jack's family had laid firm roots here in England. His forebears had set up home there centuries before – perhaps his family had always been there, since time began? There was a sense of solidarity about them, like some impenetrable glue bound them together, and I wondered whether this was why I was initially attracted to him – perhaps I had hoped that his roots could become mine, providing the stability I had craved for but had never felt as a child.

As industrial progress was made, Jack's branch of the family moved from Long Compton to Birmingham to find work. The small village could no longer support their expanding family, and Jack's father Edwin told me it was literally a case of drawing straws to see which of his generation would leave Long Compton – him or one of his brothers. In the end it was him, but he didn't mind, he had been ripe for adventure anyway (perhaps it was Edwin who Henry had inherited his desire to travel from?). So when the time had come for Jack's parents Edwin and Mary-Ann to leave the village with their children – including Jack and his brothers, they had done so quite willingly. To the vast expanse of the widening City of Birmingham they had arrived with few belongings, but with a desire to make a happy, fruitful life for themselves and their offspring.

We were living in a new era under the reign of King George V, who had inherited the throne after his father Edward VII's death in 1910; the shadow of Queen Victoria had become a distant memory since her own death in 1901. At the time of the national mourning of Queen Victoria, my family had still been in India and we heard about the news from Father's morning newspaper. I clearly remember him lifting his head momentarily and saying to Mother, 'Victoria's dead, Dear.' At which, she simply nodded in acknowledgement as he lowered his head to read the rest of the article.

Jack was one of ten children, but three of his siblings had died when they were just babies. They were very difficult times, and although the government was starting to make changes to help people who were in need of help, the living conditions were very poor and diseases like tuberculosis were rife.

By the time Jack and me got married George and Agnes were already settled down with their family and George was working for the local Shakehouse Painting Company. He had been in the armed forces but had left once his allotted time was done, and he had become a part of the reservists instead. Agnes had been resistant about giving up her job when she married and, while she did stay at home much of the time to look after the girls, she relished the times when her mother needed her help at the shop. I can remember how I used to sit watching her girls Aggie and Frances playing in the back garden of their Granny Jelfs' general store, and how I longed for the time when I would have children of my own. I wanted mine and Jack's lives to be blessed just like theirs was. But they had had their troubles and their own firstborn had died shortly after birth: a little baby boy. At the time they had naturally been virtually inconsolable. Child mortality was commonplace then, and when we look back at how many children did die, it's as though they're all as one – a statistic, but they were real, tiny, beautiful bundles to each woman. Agnes had carried the baby inside her for nine months; anticipated his birth, known him and loved him; and to lose him was utterly devastating for her.

The day of our wedding could not come soon enough. All of us women got to work making dresses and working out ways to style our hair. Even back then we were particular about such things. My younger sister, Leah, was only eight and was desperate to be my bridesmaid and follow me down the aisle with a bouquet of flowers. She had pestered and pestered me for days – how could I refuse? I made her a dress out of the same cream satin material as mine. I wore a lace-frilled high necked collar with small satin buttons down the front. Leah's was a shorter dress, which came to just below her knees – mine was almost down to my ankles, and Leah had a beautiful yellow ribbon tied around her waist with one in her hair to match. She looked so pretty.

As the day got nearer we could hardly contain our excitement. George and Florrie were going to be the witnesses to our marriage, and all our other brothers and sisters and their partners were going to be there to celebrate with us. We couldn't believe how much everyone was looking forward to this event. We couldn't have been happier if we had been King and Queen of the entire United Kingdom.

On Christmas Eve I awoke with a start. For a moment I couldn't remember where I was, and at first I felt alarmed. When I finally recalled what day it was, and that *this* was the day I would be marrying Jack, my tummy filled with butterflies, and I leapt across the room to wake Florrie and Leah. All apprehensive thoughts behind me, the three of us rushed eagerly down the stairs, creating a flurry of excitement in our wake, as my brothers, William, Thomas and little Samuel, came charging along behind us.

William was by then already working with me at the metal works factory, Thomas was just a boy of twelve and still at school. Sweet, darling Samuel was a tiny toddler and was already making his voice heard – he could be a bit of a handful at times for our mother, but his cute smile and equally appealing ways made everyone adore him, and he got away with a lot of things for which the rest of us would most certainly have been told off.

Over breakfast, not that my nerves would allow me to eat anything, we all chattered away, hardly taking a breath. Mother was her usual composed self, and Father, who was usually stoic and unresponsive, normally preferring the company of his newspaper than having to communicate with the rest of us, could hardly stop himself from joining in the laughter. It was beautiful; warm, and strangely, well, comfortable.

Upstairs, as she slowly brushed my hair and made it gleam, Florrie suddenly began to cry. As I tried to console her she blurted out that she thought everything would change from then; that it would never be like it had been. She was a nervous wreck. I really thought she would never stop crying. You would have thought we were moving hundreds of miles away instead of just two streets. I stood up and gripped hold of her tightly, hugging her and reassuring her, 'Don't be so daft, Florrie. You and me? We shall always be together.' Holding back further tears, she took a deep, deep breath and smiled, apologising for her foolishness.

When we were all dressed up and ready to go, I stole one last look in the mirror before we left, inhaled deeply, and followed Father out through the front door.

As we made our way to the street, I could see there were hordes of neighbours outside lining my route to the carriage – all waiting to wave to me as we advanced through the chilly December air. There was a dusting of snow lying like confetti on the ground, and I mused for a moment and allowed myself a smile as I considered how apt that was. Father was nervous – I hadn't seen him like that before. I suppose I was the first daughter to be married, the first child, in fact, so it was all new to him. To faraway continents he may have travelled and wars he may have fought, but on my wedding day he showed his vulnerable side.

Saint Nicolas' Church was shrouded in snow when we arrived – it looked exquisite and I should have been in awe of its beauty, but the cold air bit at my face. It made me shiver and I pulled my shawl tightly around my shoulders. Christmas Eve – it had become a tradition for our family to have December weddings, and who were we to break the mould? It was fanciful, magnificent and romantic. Nothing was going to spoil my day.

With Father at my side, and Florrie and Leah ready to walk behind me, we gathered outside the tall, arched doors waiting for the organist to give us our cue to begin walking down the aisle.

When we heard the wedding march drifting through the doors of the church doors, I clutched hold of Father's arm and began to walk slowly down the aisle. I felt faint and wished I had eaten something, but then I saw Jack waiting for me with George at his side. I took in the sea of faces – they were all smiling, and I thought, '*This is it, my perfect day.*' Jack looked so very smart; he had on a new suit and a fashionable, round-collared shirt. His tie was neatly tied into the hollow of his neck and his hair was shining, a tribute to the pomade wax he had obviously applied especially for the occasion. When I reached his side I could see reflected in his eyes the glow of the Christmas candles which had been neatly arranged all around the church ready for the Christmas services. We said our vows to each other, and because we had rehearsed them so many times in the preceding weeks, they passed without either of us faltering. Jack had been so worried, you see, worried that he would say the wrong thing and be embarrassed. But he was fine – we were both just fine.

At one point we must have gone through to sign the register, but for some reason that whole part of the wedding is a blur. I know we did, because we have the certificate showing Florrie and George's names as witnesses. Maybe I was so caught up in the event that after we'd said our vows, the important bit for me was over, and so everything until we got back to the house to celebrate is just less significant in the recesses of my mind.

Everyone came back to my parents' house to celebrate. Jack's brothers and his sister, Beck, were there. She had been known as Beck since she was a tiny girl. Before she was born their parents had lost a daughter, also called Rebecca. I suppose in the end it was less morbid to call her by the name Beck rather than by the name of the dead sister she had never met. A lot of working class people who lost their babies used to recycle their names – I have often wondered whether there was a belief that by doing so you would protect the second child? That the same thing couldn't possibly happen again?

While the grown-ups gathered around the sitting room clutching tea plates piled high with fancy cakes we had made, my sister Leah, still adorning her pretty dress, set to work at organising games for her two protégés, George and Agnes' two girls – Agnes junior who must have been three or four at the time, and Frances, who was not much more than a baby. She was walking, though, so I imagine she would have been about one or two. Leah was encouraging them to play with hoops and bouncing balls in the hallway, and we could hear chuckles and laughter echoing around the house. Hearing all the fun going on, Jack's youngest brother Frank, and my youngest brother Samuel, went to join them. It was lovely, and there was such a sense of belonging that I never wanted that day to end.

Later that day, Jack and me went to our own house a few streets away so we could spend the rest of Christmas Eve and then Christmas morning on our own. On Christmas afternoon we all met up again for Christmas Day; it was as though all of the celebrations which happened that year were just for us – Jack and Grace – the happy couple; we were like two separate beings who had become one unit. Nothing we did in our future together would be done without considering the feelings of the other, and that was a big commitment for us both to make.

We missed Jack's brother Henry that Christmas – his desire to travel had finally overtaken his need to remain with the rest of us in the Midlands. Even the prospect of a big party at home to celebrate mine and

Jack's wedding did not stop him from heading off on his way. It was sad to see him go, but in May, shortly after Jack and I had announced we were to get married, he packed his things and went down to Southampton to catch a boat to America. It was a few months before he wrote home to Edwin and Mary-Ann to let them know he was safe. Strangely, he had arrived in, not America, but Canada – Quebec to be precise. Although he was thousands of miles away, their worry was over, and they took great comfort in knowing he was happy and finally doing the adventurous things he had so longed for. Apparently he had found work 'making candy', drawing on the experiences he had gained when he had worked in Bournville. He said he still intended to go to America, but that he had missed the boat and so, on a whim, thought that at least the boat to Canada would get him to the right side of the world. His will to become an intrepid explorer had succeeded.

Just months after our wedding I began to feel sick in the mornings; I confided this revelation to Agnes and she was sure this was it; that I really was pregnant, and we talked about how once the baby was born we would take the children to the park together. Florrie was still not married at this stage and I think some of the time she felt left out – just as she had feared, my marriage to Jack had driven a wedge between us, however hard I had tried for it not to. I made a promise to myself that I would start to include her more in things I did, but in the meantime I had this possible pregnancy to contend with. Jack noticed I wasn't feeling well, but I don't think that at first he put two and two together. He was working hard at the factory and was a little distracted by that and, anyway, he used to leave the house before the nausea and sickness reached its full daily crescendo. When the sickness hadn't subsided within a month or two and was only happening in the mornings, I decided to tell him.

He was so happy about the pregnancy and the prospect of being a father. I wish so much I could go back and capture the moment that I told him. There are those times in your life which you have to save to brighten your days when things are not so good, and that is one of my 'saved moments'. When I close my eyes I can see the look of recognition on his face and how his expression of initial worry melted into sheer joy. Indeed, those are the times you want to save and remember for the whole of your life.

I thought the sickness was never going to go away, but then one day it didn't happen – it had gone as quickly as it had arrived, and I was so glad, because then I could look forward to the time when my baby arrived. I used to walk up to meet Jack from work each day, and as the baby got bigger, and I got plumper and plumper, the hill to the village green became a challenge, but I managed it – every day.

And then, as I saw Jack walking towards me, my heart used to leap with joy. This was what I had always wanted: the husband, the family, security, stability and complete and utter happiness. Sometimes Jack would have a small bar of chocolate with him – a bar that was 'spoilt' which his manager had told him to take to give to 'that pregnant wife' of his. We couldn't afford to buy chocolate, so this was a great treat. The chocolate didn't have anything wrong with it – not a break, nor a crack. It was perfect. I think Jack's manager had a soft spot for him, or perhaps he'd seen me struggling up that hill every day to meet Jack and thought I needed a little more food to sustain me through my pregnancy.

I loved those walks up the hill and along the lanes. It's so busy now, but back then there were far fewer vehicles, and the clip clop of the horses' hooves was far more regular than the sounds of motor cars. Every now and then a car would pass by me and blow its horn, or a cart pulled by two chestnut horses would pass by with cheery Mr. Whitehouse sat at its helm, and he would tip his flat cap and ask me where I was going. I would tell him, and he would get me to hop up for a ride as he was going my way. Even if he wasn't going my way he would gently turn the horses and change the direction in which he was heading. As I rode up next to him with my hair pulled back so I could feel the wind on my face, I could smell the mixed scents of lilac, roses and fresh green herbs as they lingered in the summer air. He chatted non-stop to me about Mrs. Whitehouse and their children, while in the back of the cart his old, grey-faced, black and white collie dog scampered about searching for any scraps left from his master's lunch.

When the baby decided to arrive, well, honestly, Florence was not going to make it easy for me. I thought my body was going to break, but eventually, after almost a full day, out she came, and immediately I saw her dark eyes and beautiful soft skin, I knew this was what life was all about. I would nurture her and love her until the day I died – for that was the way of things; parents died before their children did – or that was the way it was supposed to be.

Florence was born at home into a world in which the government had begun to make great changes to the welfare system – positive changes which meant that children had become healthier and, through a greater realisation that children should be entitled to a childhood, there was a greater emphasis on their education.

In addition, they started to give free health checks for all school children and, at last, death rates for diseases like measles, scarlet fever, whooping cough and tuberculosis had all fallen dramatically to around half that which we had experienced back in the times of Victoria.

Taking care of Florence in this new, much more optimistic, Britain was the easiest thing in the world for me. That feeling of fearful dread wrapped up in absolute devotion was almost intoxicating, but I think it's probably what kept me calm and able to cope. Each time I watched over her while she slept, I knew this whole thing, motherhood, just had to be right; what could be more natural? She was a tiny bundle devoid of speech or true communication – all she could request from me was my heart and that was what I gave to her. I was the one person who had to protect her and nurture her into becoming the woman she would eventually be. Women had done this since people first walked on this earth, and now it was my turn.

Over the weeks that followed she developed her own little personality, and would chuckle and laugh in what appeared to be the right places. At other times, she would scream as loud as her lungs would allow, whenever she disapproved of, or needed, something. She demanded my love and affection and I gave it willingly. It was as though before her arrival in this world I had not been truly alive.

Jack's role in my life became second place. He became the provider, the one who would get up each morning, eat the breakfast I had carefully made for him, and then, once he had gone to work, I involved Florence in all my day's chores, and relished in the quiet times we could spend alone together. It was our time.

In February 1914, as the snowdrops were poking their heads through the February snow and the buds were attempting to push their way out of the dark, dry branches, my mother died. She was just forty-four years old and had been ill for a few months and, because of my new baby she hadn't wanted to bother me with her 'woes'. When she finally told me she thought she was dying, I had only a short time to prepare myself for her death – she had cancer and it took her so quickly. I grieved for myself at her loss and I grieved for my child who would never know her wonderful grandmother.

Months passed, and while I found it difficult to concentrate at times because everything I did reminded me of my sweet, gentle, loving mother, my tiny baby grew into something resembling a small human-child, and eventually, like her ancestors before her, she was able to sit up and start to explore her environment. She began to make sounds which could have been words, and I spoke back to her as though we both understood what the other was saying. We had endless 'conversations' about food, flowers, dogs and cats we came across in the street, the weather, the world – and she would listen intently to my ramblings, mirroring my smiles and puzzled looks with those of her own.

With all of us living just a few streets from one another, we got together with our families as often as we could. The two families – the Holmes' and the Cogbills had become as one and were interchangeable. The men went to work and, for the most part, the women stayed at home and looked after the children and kept the houses in order, washing and preparing food. Life had settled into a comfortable routine.

But the world itself was changing and as the year progressed, the newspapers and the billboards echoed rumblings of news which indicated that this peace – this mini-heaven that the three of us had created – was at threat. People began whispering that Britain could be heading towards a war. There had been talk of goings-on in Europe, but it hadn't interested me. I was too busy looking after my baby. Everyone was trying hard to pass it off as being something that would blow over but, as we sat listening to the news, I could feel my heart pounding in my chest.

At the beginning of August, when Florence was just over eight months old, the hushed whispers people were making behind closed doors, the words on everyone's lips, about the possibility of an impending war became more urgent – everyone was anxious, as though there was some virulent storm on the horizon. Men were taking different stances to the news; some were insistent that they would do anything they could to protect our country; others were quieter and keeping their thoughts well hidden. Jack was like that – he became forlorn and pensive. I felt as though I couldn't quite reach him. Where before once he had eaten his dinner he would play and laugh with Florence until it was time for her to go to bed, by then he had become on edge, and was more likely to sit with a newspaper in front of him, taking in each word, waiting for news of what was happening. 'Surely Prime Minister Asquith will let us all know what is going on,' he repeatedly muttered to the space in front of him.

'Just settle, Jack, perhaps it will all just blow over – there's no point in worrying yourself about things that might never happen,' I reassured him.

It wasn't long, however, before it was confirmed that we were, indeed, at war with Germany.

Within a few days everyone's life descended into desperate turmoil. It didn't matter where a person was from, or what position they held in life, at this point everyone was in shock. No one really knew what would happen next. Few people really understood the consequences of what we were hearing on the news and seeing in the newspapers. Who were we at war with? Why were we at war? Were we going to be invaded? What was the government expecting from us? Questions, so many questions, and yet, if answers came they were never very clear.

Lord Kitchener, the newly-appointed Secretary of State for War, very quickly let us know what was going to happen. The men who were eligible and who had a military background were to leave immediately. There was little time for loved ones to say goodbye before they had to go.

Agnes was devastated when she discovered George would have to gather up a few meagre belongings and take them with him. No time for reflection, no time to make plans for the future. He was to join the rest of the 3rd Worcestershires and be mobilised immediately.

While George and the other men waited to embark for France they were based at Warwickshire cricket ground, and Agnes was able to see him fleetingly just one more time when she took the girls down there and asked if George's two daughters would be able to see their father before he left. The officials at the gates were reluctant, but Agnes' pleading appealed to their softer sides and George came out for just twenty minutes and said farewell to the three of them. It was all so fast. One minute they were a close-knit family, and the next he was no longer with them.

By mid-August he and his battalion had already crossed the English Channel into France.

I am ashamed to say that I was no use to Agnes – not then anyway. I helped her with the girls, but I was so caught up in my own fear that Jack, too, would have to leave, that I didn't help her as much as I should have. She was like an extra sister to me, our children were cousins, but I was so wrapped up in me that it was hard for me to comprehend someone else's suffering.

My father, as much as he wanted to go to defend his country, well, by then he was in his late forties and he was too old to go to war. Instead, he got on with running the public house he had recently bought – the motor trade he had entered after leaving the army had become too exhausting for him, and he liked the attention he got from being a pub landlord.

Our men were going to have to go and stop this enemy from invading our country and pillaging our homes. That was the plan, and there was nothing any of us could do about it. I couldn't equate how we would cope without Jack if he had to go away. Where would the money come from? What about his job at the chocolate factory? It makes me ashamed now to think of how trivial that may sound, but being rational is not a part of war, and as time went by we came to realise that. It was as though the whole world had been thrown into a state of turmoil. No one seemed to know what their role was any more – whether they were working, going off to fight, or just staying at home and waiting for someone to let them know what they had to do next.

In the beginning, however, it worked out that Jack was to stay home for the meantime – he was to remain as part of the reserve army until such time as they told him otherwise. Initially they were simply taking volunteers for the forces. I felt guilty to be so relieved. My Jack was safe because he had me and Florence; he and millions like him were given special dispensation because they had a family. In the end, at that point anyway, it was the luck of the draw, or whether you had ever been involved in the military before, which dictated whether or not you had to go.

Father, having been to war before, was extremely knowledgeable about these things. He reassured us by saying that the government would sort it out and that everything would be okay. He said something about not letting the enemy get away with it, but I didn't really understand what he meant. I didn't know, couldn't comprehend, why we had gone to war – it all seemed so complex. I knew there had been an assassination in Sarajevo – Franz Ferdinand, who was the heir to the Austro-Hungarian throne, and his wife, had been killed by a young man called Gavrilo Princip at the end of June, but surely all this hadn't escalated because of that? I knew that Belgium had been invaded by German forces, and that on 4th August we had declared war on Germany.

What did we, here in Britain, have to do with all that? Were we like cart horses and blinkered so we couldn't see what was going on around us? Was our whole nation tricked into a war which none of us fully understood?

Surely this would all be over by Christmas – that is what everyone was saying anyway, and I hoped they would be right, and that Agnes would soon have George back home with her.

Agnes and George Cogbill

Before the war, George Cogbill front centre

Jack Cogbill (1912)

William Holmes in 1895 with his first medal

Chapter 2

Off to War

There were posters everywhere – in shop windows, on billboards in the street – people even attached them to their garden walls; a massive publicity campaign had been established very quickly reminding people that Kitchener wanted volunteers to come and join the army. The war was happening, it really was, and men, including George, had already left for the continent. The country needed more men to sign up – there was no way we were going to miss that fact. We were being encouraged to stand up for what was right by casting away any fears and 'doing the right thing'. Our country needed more soldiers and Kitchener made sure we had that thought securely wedged in our minds. The posters had Kitchener pointing at us as he quite explicitly told us 'Your Country Needs You'.

In the newspaper there were articles telling us women that if our men didn't go and sign up then they were cowards – cowards who did not deserve us. They informed us that we should not pity the girl whose man had gone to war – he wasn't just fighting for her, he was also fighting for us. Strangely enough, it had been we working classes who had been quickest to respond and, eventually, the middle and upper classes were shamed into doing their 'bit', and newspaper articles began to reflect this situation.

There was so much pressure on everyone – men to go and sign up, and women to force their men to go and sign up. They were very difficult, troubled times and so many of us were at risk of being publicly humiliated.

The white feather became a symbol of cowardice and men who were eligible to go, but who didn't volunteer, were handed them in the street, or they were put inside envelopes and posted through their front doors. It was so awful, but the strength of feeling was desperate, and the emotions we were all experiencing were daunting. I don't think anyone really knew quite what they were doing, and I suppose now, looking back from more than three decades on, that's what allowed us to eventually forgive one another.

With George gone to France and no news of how he was, the family fell into a state of disarray. By September things were becoming quite desperate – no one could ignore the messages – they were *everywhere* you went, and any man without dependents who appeared to be fit enough was forced into acting on his conscience and making his way to whichever rendezvous had been advertised. It was voluntary at this stage. Voluntary, they said, but it most certainly was not. Woe betided any man who ignored the whisperings as people passed them by in the street or in the local shop. There was no escape from it –

unless you were to become a 'CO' – conscientious objectors they were known as, and they were ostracised and sometimes imprisoned for their beliefs.

What none of us ever expected was that Jack's brother Edwin Junior would react to the pressure and take it upon himself to go and sign up. He secretly responded to Kitchener's call for young men who had no ties to go and fight but, at just seventeen, he was officially too young to go. He was not unlike Jack to look at – just a younger version, but he had this determination, a stubbornness which drove him on.

'Boy soldiers', that's what they called boys like Edwin – boys who joined the army by lying about their age. To join up he should really have been eighteen, and then to go to the continent, he should have been nineteen, but somehow these boys got through – they passed their fitness tests and foiled the authorities. Was this what the government had wanted? Young boys to go and fight the wars of men?

It is possible these boys went to sign up through a genuine desire to keep Britain free from this monstrous impending enemy invasion we had all begun to anticipate, or maybe it was because of their need to not be seen as being cowardly? Whatever it was, the families back home had to remain behind and pick up the pieces resulting from their absence.

Jack's mother, Mary-Ann, was beside herself with

despair when, as we were all having soup and bread there one afternoon in September, we discovered what Edwin had done, but Edwin Senior told her that 'Junior' was all but a man and that it was his duty. He duly patted Edwin on the head and said 'Well done, Son, we're very proud of you.'

Mary-Ann immediately fell silent. What could she do? Her voice had been overridden by her husband's, and while Edwin was normally such a gentle character, this war we had been flung into instilled in us all patriotic passions which we normally would not have contemplated. Mary-Ann later confided in me that she had wanted to go to the authorities, but the abject disrespect of going against Edwin Senior outweighed the fear of her son leaving. It was a travesty that so many women were quietened by their husbands into consenting to give their sons up to a war none of us understood.

In years to come, when we had had plenty of time to reflect on the war and all that had happened, we became aware that, compared to some, Edwin was relatively old. Some boys who went away were just fourteen or fifteen years old. Everyone knew this was happening – how could we not have known? We had seen these boys grow up, watched them change from chubby babies into cheeky boys, and then become handsome teenagers disguised as men.

But underneath all their bravado they were still just

boys – even Edwin.

I worried about my own brothers: Samuel was the youngest and still a small boy – just four years old when the war broke out, William was twenty, although because of Father having the same name, we all called him Bill. He used to spend his time going to the library to read books and research natural remedies. He was always telling people what was good for them. Word got around that he was some kind of medicine-man and everyone used to come to him back in those days when they had an ailment and say things like, 'Look here, young Bill, I've got this little lump on my knee, what do you think I should do about that?' And off they would go with a remedy he had concocted for them. He wasn't a doctor or anything, but I think he should have been, as very few of his 'patients' came back to complain that his medicine had not worked. Thomas, who had been born just at the end of the 1800s, was just fifteen and was desperate to follow in Father's footsteps, but in spite of this, Father told him to just bide his time. If Father had let him get away with it, though, Thomas would have followed Edwin to war – even then, when he was just fifteen years old.

Father never spoke of what he had seen and done in the Boer War. When we lived overseas he and Mother had had photographs up on the living room wall of him posing with all his medals emblazoned across the jacket of his uniform, but he kept all his thoughts close to his chest. There was also a picture of him posing with his Boer War comrades – Father had his hand resting on a large, smooth-coated bulldog-type dog's head, but he never told us anything about the people in the picture – or the dog. He was a private, and sometimes quite bossy, man and I felt that Mother had always been on her guard when she was talking to him. He could be quite irritable with her, but then at other times he was so gentle and kind. He used to bring her beautiful jewellery and smart new clothes in rich colours, and she would hold them up against her and say, 'Look at this, Gracie, look at what your wonderful father has bought for me.' And then she would look over at him, smile and add, 'Thank you, My Dearest – you are the kindest man in the world.' He would nod in acknowledgement and suck on his pipe or cigar, inhale deeply, and then breathe the smoke out from under his moustache. I think he missed having someone on whom to bestow gifts like that after Mother died, and we all expected that he wouldn't stay without a wife for very long.

After he left the army, Father had joined the motor trade, but he had found it physically exhausting and managed to secure a lease on a pub, and our house was attached to the side of it. Over the counter he used to sell clay pipes which were about a foot long. A lot of people smoked them in those days. Before the war William and Thomas worked for Father lifting barrels up out of the basement and carrying them up to the bar. Father had been affected by the wars he had seen and he didn't have a lot of patience. He used to get very cross with the boys and was very short tempered. Whether it really was what he had seen and what he had been through, or whether that was just his way, I don't know, but he was like that a lot. He had a face that he showed to the customers and one that he showed to his family. I often thought that perhaps Mother should have left him, but it was nearly impossible in those days – even today it is so very difficult, but it was extremely rare back then.

Almost as soon as the war began, the government introduced a Defence of the Realm Act (otherwise known as DORA), which all civilians were to abide by. It was as though our lives as individuals had become second place as we all rose up and defended our country as one. We were not allowed to talk in public about the armed forces or anything to do with our defence system. We weren't allowed to purchase binoculars or alcohol in railway stations, and we weren't allowed to light any bonfires. The government was able to take over land and buildings at their own volition and, I suppose, to all intents and purposes, we all became part of the government's property. Some of these new rules seemed almost bizarre, but rules were rules, and we had no option but to abide by them.

We packed our sandwiches and went to see Edwin as he and his battalion, the 1st/14th Battalion of the Royal Warwickshire Regiment, had the last of their many marches through the town centre. They marched past the cathedral and people cheered and shouted. There were so many young men, and with them all dressed in uniform with very short haircuts, it was difficult for anyone to pick out their own loved ones, but then suddenly, Edwin Senior shouted, 'Look, Mary-Ann, look over there! There's our boy!'

We all looked to where he was pointing and, sure enough, there was Junior. We all waved to him and, as he marched past us, we witnessed him allowing himself the tiniest of smiles. Edwin and Mary-Ann were very proud that day, but I couldn't help thinking how much Junior had looked as though he was just a young lad dressed up in the clothes of a soldier – as though he were heading off to a fancy dress parade.

The 'Pals' they called them. They were regiments made up of groups of young men from particular areas or from various professions; friends or acquaintances who knew one other. Kitchener had realised that it would be worth encouraging particular groups of men to join up together, as that would instil an immediate sense of camaraderie which otherwise would not exist, or at least would have taken longer to foster with people who had not known each other before the war. While what Kitchener instigated did actually work, in the long run it was to turn out to be a quite catastrophic strategy, because a hit on a particular regiment became a hit on a particular area or group of people, and sometimes whole streets of boys were affected with complete communities being devastated by their loss.

News began to filter back to us about life in the trenches and we learned that men we had known were losing their lives. There was a man called Arthur who lived in our street who had come back from the war shortly after it began. He had to spend months in hospital until, finally, one day he returned home. He had lost half of one leg and the foot of his other. No one knew what to say to him. His wife had to push him around in a chair, and he was a big chap. He used to sit in the chair mumbling about the war, and it was only when you got over the fact that he was missing a leg, and you really started to listen to him, that you began to absorb the terror of what he had been through.

He was sitting outside in the sun one day where his wife had deposited him in his wheelchair. He told me she'd said it was so she could have a bit of peace and quiet. I felt sorry for him, so I had gone over to speak to him to find out how he was getting on. In great detail he told me the whole story about his life in the trenches and of how the men were hungry, frightened, and dirty. There had been an unexpected attack and they had to prepare quickly to go 'over the top'. He said he had been hit by a bullet, and before he had known what was happening he had found himself lying on the ground with the putrid stench of death all around him. The smell had filled his senses making him wretch; his heart had throbbed heavily against his chest as he had looked down at his legs and seen the damage that had been done. He felt faint and drifted in and out of consciousness thinking this was it; he was going to die. But then, in the distance he heard someone calling his name. This other soldier then dragged him to safety back in the trenches on the Allies' side of No Man's Land. He was safe from further harm, but he would never run again; never walk again without assistance.

After that day I made a point of talking to Arthur whenever I saw him. Each time we spoke he told me the same story and it never changed, except for the peripheral things that had happened, you know, like the conditions which affected them all: the rats scurrying around their feet, all set on their own agenda – little creatures with their own plans for survival; the lice which invaded the men's hair and fed from their tender red scalps; the boredom – when days would pass without anything happening; the smoking which abated the boredom but which made them cough weary coughs; the mud which filled their boots and covered their rancid clothes. Arthur knew I had always had a soft spot for animals and told me that beyond the trenches the horses were suffering and everyone knew this, but no one had done anything about it. He used to see horses up to the tops of their legs in mud and struggling to walk on hooves that were unshod and living on a meagre diet that was insufficient for the arduous work they were meant to be undertaking. Their lives had become entangled with the lives of the men and neither had any choice about being there. These were the horses that the government had bought from ordinary people – they used to be carthorses and children's pets – they were not tools of conflict. It was as though this damned war and all its misery had removed any sense of humanity, dignity and morality.

These were all topics of conversation Arthur should not really have been talking to me about, and he always did so in a quiet voice in case he was overheard. Before starting to speak he would glance from side to side and look behind him, he would then cup his hand halfway around his mouth and lean in towards me. I think it helped him being able to talk about it. They were terrible experiences the men were expected to hold inside them.

I noticed that Jack invariably avoided walking past Arthur's house, to the extent that he would walk around the block the other way to avoid doing so. I challenged him about it, and he said he found it difficult to equate that his brothers had gone off to face the situations that Arthur was describing, and he felt guilty. He was in the army reserve, but for the time being he continued to work at the chocolate factory. He was also frightened that his brothers might return home in the same predicament as poor old Arthur, and he couldn't cope with that fear; he couldn't deal with confronting an image of that possibility.

Jack's brother, Alfred, and my brother, Bill, had stayed at home for a while too because their skills as metalworkers were necessary in helping to develop the munitions factories, but then they both received letters informing them they had to go and sign up. I was visiting Jack's parents with Florence and sitting next to their living room fire when Alfred's letter arrived. Mary-Ann's face became white. Naively, she had thought that because he was fully employed at the munitions factory, he wouldn't have to go, but war is not logical, and shortly after that, off he went.

It transpired they had called him up because the skills he had were going to be equally useful at The Front, and by then they had begun to employ women to do the jobs of men in the factories. Alfred's sweetheart, Ellen, became one of those young women. Ellen was beautiful – petite with blue eyes and dark curls which framed her face. They worked together for a little while, and she missed him when he had gone. She used to come and visit me to sit and talk about Alfred and to play with Florence. She was a sweet young thing and completely besotted by Alfred.

Eventually, my brother Bill left to go to India – his skills were needed in the Commonwealth. I saw him before he went away and he left me with a list of herbal medicines I could create should any of us become sick. Of all of the men who left, Bill was the one I worried least about – he was a survivor. He had a gentle, determined, yet sensible, way about him which people warmed to, and I felt he would be able to talk his way out of every crisis he came across, either that or use his knowledge to create and barter remedies. In times of war, people needed folk like Bill – particularly if they came bearing medicines.

And so, it very quickly emerged that apart from young Frank, who was still too young to go to fight, Jack would be the only one of his brothers left behind, and while this bothered him, I was relieved he was still at home, as was his poor mother, Mary-Ann. My brother Tom was still at home, but his interest in the forces worried me, and I hoped he wouldn't go off and do anything foolish.

Jack had begun having some strange symptoms, though. Sometimes he would be sitting reading a newspaper, and I would notice his face twitch. It alarmed me, and I told him so, but he wasn't aware of it. And then, when he was sleeping, he would occasionally have what I would now refer to as convulsions, and he would wake me up with his thrashing about in the bed. He would not see the doctor, although I insisted many a time. He said he had been having nightmares and that the doctors would not take him seriously – but to me it seemed as though it was something much more than nightmares he was having.

While they said the war would be over by Christmas, it wasn't, and Agnes grew more and more worried and frustrated about George not being at home. It was difficult for me to console her – how could I empathise when my dear Jack was still by my side?

Weeks turned into months and one morning I felt those same old feelings of nausea return. At first the penny didn't drop, but as the same feeling occurred over the following days, always as I was waking up, I realised what was happening. Even so, I couldn't quite grasp the thought that I might be pregnant, and for several weeks I was in a persistent state of denial. As he had when I had Florence, Jack didn't notice, he just thought I was worried about the war and what was happening to our brothers. When I realised there was no doubt whatsoever that I was, indeed, having another baby, one evening after he had eaten his broth and the meagre quantity of bread and potatoes I had served him for dinner, I told him. I didn't know what reaction to expect, and at first he was quiet, but then he half smiled and reached out to hug me. No words, just comfort. Neither of us knew what to say; our actions substituted our words.

How could we even begin to think of bringing a child into that disordered, frenzied, messed up world? I would lie awake in the darkest hours feeling my belly, waiting for some sign that my baby was okay. Every now and then I would feel a gentle kick; a flutter of life, and while with Florence that feeling had given me hope, this time I felt a desolate foreboding. While I longed for my dream to come true that with new life there would be new beginnings, the desperate feelings in the pit of my stomach would not go away. The night times were the worst, because at least during the day I could share my worries with Jack's mum and Agnes. Florrie had become very distant, she had found herself a young man who by that time was already away to war, and I think she found it difficult to be around me because I had Florence and Jack was still at home. When I told her I was pregnant again she became aloof and disinterested – the separation between us she had feared would happen was becoming more of a reality and I felt it was out of my control.

Christmas 1914 was a desperate affair, with no one feeling like celebrating. Too many people had too many worries, and we all went to church and prayed and then returned home for a small lunch, but it was hard knowing that there were so many missing from our lives. At least we were hopeful that the war wouldn't possibly still be going on by the following Christmas. Eventually these optimistic thoughts consoled us, and all talk turned to what we would be doing the following year when we were all reunited.

For the first time I felt I could imagine the four of us together in the hub of our extended families: me, Jack, Florence, and the new baby.

Chapter 3

1915

Our Christmas optimism was short-lived and with great haste the war was edging closer to us. There were reports of strange objects in the sky over the east coast of England. They were identified as airships and known as Zeppelins after the person who invented them. There were pictures of them in all the newspapers, along with images of the devastation they had reaped. People were suddenly in fear of their own lives, which added to the intense worry many already had about their sons and husbands on the continent.

At that point we didn't know the true capability of the Zeppelins. For all we had known they could have been far more effective at hurting people than they eventually turned out to be. In Birmingham, being about as far as you can get away from the sea, for the most part we were protected from any invasion by these objects, but they did darken the skies over the Midlands on a few occasions during the war. They were certainly persistent, I'll give them that.

By now Florence was walking well and she had begun to form proper sounds which, with a stretch of the imagination, sounded like words. I chatted away to her as I had done before, but now to my great joy, she would reciprocate. As July and the birth of the baby drew nearer, I started to tell Florence about how she would soon have a tiny brother or sister.

Each day when I had prepared Jack's dinner ready for him to come home, she and I would walk to meet him from work. On the way we would pass a small shop where we could find the best bread I have ever tasted – fresh from the oven. Mr. Curtis used to bake all day long, even that late on in the day and, because I had a craving for bread, I could hardly pass the shop without going in to chat to him.

I tried to time my passing the shop for the moment when he was actually at the point of lifting the tray of fresh, fragrant bread and rolls out of the oven, and I would stand talking to him while I inhaled the blend of baked flour and yeast as it lingered; the bread cooling in the air. With Florence sat balanced on the edge of the counter, with me holding onto her, Mr. Curtis would lean over to her and say, 'Do you want some nice, warm bread, little Flo?' and Florence would giggle at him as he broke off a small piece of loaf and placed it in her tiny hand. Then he would hold the remaining loaf up in front of him and add, 'Golly me, would you just take a look at that, I can't possibly sell that bread now.' Without another word he would wrap the rest of the warm loaf in paper and, with a cheeky wink, and a smile reflected in his warm, blue eyes, pass it across the counter to me.

I ate so much bread some days I thought I would explode. Food was becoming short then, but people used to help us out because I was expecting. Everyone was lovely, and sometimes I even forgot there was a war going on, or, at least that was until about six weeks before I was due to give birth.

One lunchtime at the end of May, Agnes and I had arranged to meet on the village green with the children. It was one o' clock and some of the factories were changing their shifts. I saw a woman I used to work with standing right where the edge of the lush, emerald green grass met the path. I motioned for her to come over, which she did. She immediately told me her husband was in France and, as I paused before replying, she suddenly let out a tirade of abuse, 'How can you stand there and look so relaxed about everything? There's a war going on you know?' And then, pointing down at my belly, she spat, 'You wouldn't have THAT to look forward to if your Jack was doing his duty like other men.' And with that, she tossed her blonde tresses and marched around the corner and out of sight. I don't remember her name now, but I've never forgotten the look she had on her face that day.

Mr. Curtis had been watching out of his shop window when this altercation happened. He called Agnes, me and the children over and told me not to worry about what people think. 'These children are the ones we need to think about and look after here,' he said, 'nothing else.' He miraculously discovered three red lollipops in a jar behind the counter and deposited them one by one in each girl's eager grasp, and then we went on our way. Agnes consoled me that it was no one else's business and that there were plenty of women having babies but, still, I felt guilty.

I was terribly shaken after that encounter on the village green and became self-absorbed, wallowing in the last weeks of my pregnancy at home, hiding from everyone and only venturing out when I had to. I was waiting for my little bundle to arrive so I could take him or her out and show the world outside that there was hope. This new generation was our future and we needed to nurture and love them, not resent them for being born in a time of conflict. The more time I spent on my own while Jack was working, however, the more the old feelings from early on in my pregnancy returned, and I began to fret about bringing a baby into a world which was as troubled as that one was.

In the early hours of June 22nd my waters broke.

It was the middle of the night and I had got up to use the chamber pot. As I walked across the cold, wooden floor I felt an overwhelming urge to be sick. As I steadied myself on the bedpost, I felt a sudden bearing down, and then, 'Gush', out flowed the fluid from around the baby.

This runny, viscous substance spread itself all over

the floorboards and was seeping into the edge of the rug.

With Florence I had had some warning as the contractions had come first, but not this time. Of course, there had been some sense of contraction-like feelings, but I had thought it was too early for the baby to be born.

Jack panicked. The first time there had been enough time for him to be able to go and get help before it got to this stage, but as I screeched at him to go and get Dottie, he seemed not to be listening and was muttering about going to get a mop. I tried again as I could hear him shuffling things around down in the scullery. And then louder, with all the force of my lungs, I screeched, 'JAAAAAACK...THE MIDWIFE...GO...AND...GET...DOTTIE.' The urgency in my voice must have finally got through to him, and as I made my way onto the bed, familiar excruciating pains filled my abdomen.

When Dottie arrived I was hysterical – it had seemed to take ages for them to get back. Florence had heard all the commotion and come through to see what was going on. She was clinging to my side trying to console me in her innate, infant way, but I hardly knew she was there. Every now and then I saw the image of her tearstained face and, between contractions, I tried to hold onto her and comfort her, but when the baby was intermittently trying to force its way through there was nothing I could do but scream.

I remember reading a book which had been published about the time that Florence was born. It was all about diseases particular to women and how to have an easy childbirth. I noted all the things I was meant to do to make things go smoothly for me when my baby arrived. But everything I had learned about being of good mind and not nervous when giving birth went out of the window. The book had advised me that during my pregnancy I should go to church and places of amusement; avoid gossip; take cold sponge baths; and eat well so I wouldn't put on too much weight. It assured me that if I did all of these things then the baby would literally slither into this world. Well, whoever called childbirth 'labour', was not kidding – I was in agony, in spite of all my best intentions and that darned book.

When Jack returned with Dottie he had also brought Florrie with him. I was surprised to see her after her recent lack of interest in me or my family, but she was obviously there to help. Jack was dispatched downstairs with the almost inconsolable Florence attached to his side and told he must wait there until he was called. Florrie had been helping out at the local hospital and, while Dottie encouraged me and told me when to push, Florrie stroked my head and mopped my brow. In between times she held tightly to my hand and spoke softly to me.

'You're nearly there, Gracie, nearly there.'

All through the night and into the next day we stayed in that room with the same scenes being played out over and over again.

I was exhausted.

Jack knocked on the door at one point in the morning and Florrie and Dottie simultaneously shouted, 'Not yet, Jack'. Much later on Mary-Ann arrived and came to give me some encouragement while Florrie looked after Florence so Jack could go into work. When Jack came home from work an hour early because his boss had discovered I was in labour and had told him he should go home, the contractions were still coming. I thought the baby was never going to come out. I had heard of women who had died giving birth and I began to dread that this was going to happen to me. I worried about Florence and how she would survive without me. That thought seemed to give me the strength to carry on, and finally, with one last great push, my baby was born.

Relief flooded through my body, and within minutes I heard a weak little cry. My little baby girl was wrapped in a shawl and handed over to me. She had been a breech baby, and Dottie and Florrie later admitted that they thought I was not going to be able to give birth to her. They really had expected they were going to lose us both. I had known something was up, but I hadn't wanted to comprehend that having a baby would be something which could end my life. I wasn't ready to give up on this world.

Florence was eighteen months old when her little sister arrived in our family. Adeline Grace is the name we gave to her. Our sweet little Adeline, baby 'Adie', was born on June 23rd, just two days after my own birthday. She was my beautiful, late birthday present – my little piece of late-midsummer sunshine.

We took her out with us and showed her to everyone we knew – even some people who we didn't know, and although Florence was so young she revelled in the attention that was being given to our little family. People would come out of their houses to press coins and other good luck charms into Adeline's tiny hand. She seemed to instil a sense of hope in all who met her.

But then, one afternoon and completely out of the blue, Adeline became sick. She had a fever and started to convulse, and as we soothed her and held her tightly so she wouldn't hurt herself, before we could get a doctor to her, she was gone. When he arrived, the doctor said she was just one of the weak ones, and her difficult birth had meant that when she was born she was already exhausted. It was a warm, sunny, beautiful summer's morning when she died;

the world suddenly appeared to be in a conflicted state of war and beauty, and my baby Adeline had died in my arms; my dear, adorable little child was called back to the Heaven from which she had come such a short time before – lent to us by some force much greater than any of us could begin to imagine.

Jack went to register her birth and death at the same time, while I stayed at home and hugged my one remaining child close to me, trying to comprehend what this world had to offer, and why such cruel, dark days had taken over our lives.

In a daze of despair, we organised her funeral. We had not got much money, but the family all contributed a little so we could give her more than a pauper's funeral. Families who didn't have enough money would have to combine their child's funeral with that of an adult who had died around the same time and I didn't want that for my baby – but then, I suppose no one would. I wanted Adeline to have her own horse-drawn carriage and her own service; I had loved her for just seven days, but that love would live in me for the rest of my life. We had the funeral director make us black-rimmed funeral cards with the words "Jesus has called a little child" printed on them.

On the day, the blinkered, chestnut horses pulled the carriage to the front of our house and Adeline's tiny coffin was lifted into it. Neighbours came out into the street: men with their caps held to their chests, and ladies dressed in black with white handkerchiefs lifted to their faces. As a sign of respect each family had closed their front curtains. After the short journey to the cemetery, our whole family gathered around the tiny grave and I cried like I had never cried before. How could life go on without her? I had known her since she was a tiny being in my belly – I had anticipated a life with her, and that dream would never come to fruition. For a long time that was hard for me to come to terms with.

In the months that followed I felt guilty and alone. Jack had his own grief, his own worries to contend with. While he moped about the loss of his child, I blamed myself for not being able to give birth to her properly. I couldn't understand how I could have had one child and the birth could have been so natural, and yet with Adeline there were so many complications. People said that it was because Adeline was a weak baby and because she was breech – even the doctor told me that. They told me that a stronger baby would have been desperate to get out and would have had a better head start in life. But I found it hard to deal with and I closed myself off from people for a while, all the time wondering what I had done so wrong during my pregnancy that had made my baby die. It was only Mary-Ann who, because she had lost three of Jack's siblings, and Agnes, who had lost her firstborn, her baby boy, who really seemed to understand. I would only allow the two of them into my world – everyone else became part of my peripheral life including, at times, Jack.

My one joy, the one person on whom I could bestow all my love and affection, was Florence, and I did all that I could to make her happy.

Within weeks of Adeline's death we found a little black stray dog and named him Ted. He turned up scavenging in the yard one day. He had probably been put out on the streets by his owners when they could no longer feed him – many people had taken their animals to be euthanised at the beginning of the war. Huge queues of people had lined the streets waiting for their pets to be put to sleep through a fear of not being able to manage to feed them. This little mite had escaped that fate, and he was so small I figured he wouldn't have too big an appetite, so I persuaded Jack we should keep him. Jack was doubtful, but I pleaded, and within a few hours we had made a comfy bed for Ted in the kitchen. Very quickly he became a little playmate for Florence and, I suppose on many levels, he helped our small family in our healing.

Little by little I began to let Jack back into my life, and the three of us and our new small dog became what started to feel like a real family. During the mornings when Jack was eating his breakfast we used to talk about our plans for the day, and then at night we would reflect on what had happened and share our worries and joys. It seemed as though the war was far away when the three of us and Ted were enclosed in the confines of our domestic bliss, safely tucked inside our little terraced house.

In late October 1915 Mary-Ann and Edwin Senior received a letter saying Henry had met a girl in Canada and was getting married. It was to be a Christmas wedding. She was seven years younger than Henry and her name was Maisie. Henry's escape to his new world in Canada had proved to be the best thing he could have done – here he was marrying into a Canadian family and spending his time making 'candy'.

There was much speculation in the family that perhaps they had HAD to get married. Mary-Ann told us we were being ridiculous and was definitely fearful of the shame upon the family. She had received a lot of correspondence from Henry, and this was the first time Maisie had been mentioned, which only added fuel to the fire. We were all banned from mentioning the issue any further. Behind closed doors we continued to cast aspersions as to the likelihood that Maisie was, indeed, having a baby, even Edwin Senior joined in, but we never mentioned it again to Mary-Ann.

Not then anyway.

Edwin's regiment, the Royal Warwickshires, were still

in Britain, having spent a lot of time training in Sutton Park and in other parts of the country. In December he managed to get over to see his mother and father before he left for France and the war. Me, Jack and Florence were over there visiting them when Edwin turned up and, after a light lunch, he stood up to go. His mother went over to him and put her finger against his lips. 'Don't say 'Goodbye', Son, say to me, 'I'll see you soon'.'

Edwin smiled a boyish smile – his uniform still seeming not quite right. He hugged us each in turn, with a special big kiss on the cheek for Florence, and then turned to his mother. 'I'll see you soon, Mother'.

She cried that day.

We all cried.

In December 1915, just before Florence's second birthday, Jack received a card from the War Office telling him that he would soon receive another letter in which he would be informed of the date, time and place at which he would need to report once he was required for service. He would be given two weeks' notice. Suddenly the war that everyone else was experiencing, and which I had often felt on the periphery of, became my war. I felt my days with Jack here at home were numbered, and I saw him returning to how he had been just after his brothers had left to go and fight – he was despondent;

troubled. We took some solace in the fact that neither set of parents had been in receipt of one of those dreadful cards or letters telling them that one of their sons was missing in action or dead. But there were so many men we had known who were not returning, we felt there was only so long before one of our families was affected. It was only a matter of time before Jack would be leaving us, and each night I lay awake fretting, while Jack tossed and turned in the bed beside me, sometimes talking in his sleep and intermittently exhibiting those strange convulsing movements.

Over the following days, an idea began to germinate in my head that because he was clearly not well, Jack may be able to stay at home. I was sure that when he went for a medical he would be classed as being unfit for service. I voiced this to Jack and he became terribly cross with me: he had absolutely no intention whatsoever of admitting to any medical officer that there might be something wrong with him.

In the years that followed, I realised that it would have been a slight on his manliness; his brothers and my brother Bill were already away doing their 'bit', and as far as he was concerned he should have been there too. While he was waiting, life continued as normal; he was still there physically, but it was as though we were both balanced on the edge of a precipice – and if either of us were to fall, the other would, too.

Practically everyone we knew, their lives had been put 'on hold', we couldn't progress or make plans for the future, and we couldn't reflect on what had gone before. We were stuck in a static situation; frozen in time in a place that no longer seemed to tally with either the past or what was to come.

Chapter 4

1916

In early May, another letter arrived with news from Canada. Edwin Senior and Mary-Ann now had a new grandchild; Henry's wife, Maisie, had given birth to a baby girl.

Mary-Ann had tried to keep the birth a secret, but Edwin Senior let it slip when we were all around the old wooden table one day sipping our steaming hot tea. I could not bring myself to let my eyes meet Edwin Senior's, lest I spurt my mouthful of food all over the table in hysterics, but then, as I sat there trying to keep control of myself, I heard Beck stifle a chuckle. Oh dear, what a furore that caused, as the two of us burst out laughing. Once more we were banned from ever mentioning the subject.

Eventually, Mary-Ann displayed the photographs Henry had sent over, but it took a while. The baby was gorgeous and clearly resembled Mary-Ann – perhaps that was why she was able to forgive her beloved son for his wayward behaviour. There's no doubt that having Henry halfway across the world made it easier for her to ignore the slight three month discrepancy between his marriage and the birth of his child. There was great shame in what had happened, and I felt bad for finding his predicament amusing, and before the war we certainly would not have found it such, but we had all needed a little light relief, and in his absence poor Henry had become the focus of our wicked attention. Looking back now, I don't think that it was Henry's situation that we had found amusing – it was more Mary-Ann's steadfast denial that it could have been a possibility in the first place.

The war raged on, and in January 1916 National Conscription was introduced. By May that year it became compulsory for all men between the ages of eighteen and forty-one to join up for military service. Jack was issued with papers informing him he had to enlist for active service on May 29th. That two weeks' notice he had been informed of had arrived, and although he had been expecting it because we had seen it in the newspapers and because of the previous letter he had received back in the December, when the notice arrived it still came as a shock. This was mainly, I think, because we had pushed it to the backs of our minds and hoped the war would be over before he was called; we had continued to believe, to hope, that the war was what was happening around us, not what would actually happen to us.

Jack's letter instructed him to go to James Watt Street in Birmingham where he would complete all the forms and have the necessary medical checks. When he told me about the medicals I was secretly delighted. They couldn't possibly let him go off to fight. He was not well enough.

When the 29th arrived I was optimistic that he would not be going to war. Giving him a packed lunch which I had carefully wrapped up in paper, I bade him farewell and cheerily told him I would see him later on. He looked at me in the most puzzled way, but I couldn't articulate how I felt, because that would have meant his knowing that I thought he was going to fail the medical. There was a spring in my step as I cleaned the house and fed and entertained Florence and Ted that day.

At dinner time Jack came home, and all was not quite how I'd imagined it would be.

He *had* signed up and was to be mobilised the very next day as a gunner with the Royal Garrison Artillery (RGA). 'A gunner?' I repeated after him, astounded that he had been accepted for the forces, but not only that, that they had thought it appropriate to make him work directly with weaponry.

While Jack explained that he had completed all the forms, and went on to tell me triumphantly that he had passed the medical examination, the word 'gunner' kept on repeating itself in my mind. It was as though my brain had been taken over by some ubiquitous force which I couldn't control, until, finally, I let out a tirade: 'A *gunner* Jack! What on earth do *you* know about being a *gunner*? Gunners are people who kill people; you've never killed anyone in your life. You're my wonderful, sweet Jack who wouldn't deliberately hurt anyone – how can they turn you into a murderer?'

Jack's defences were immediately stimulated and he bit back. 'What do you think they're all doing out there, Grace? Eh? There's a war going on – they're not out there having afternoon tea and cavorting with the natives, you know!' He reached into his pocket and pulled out a small booklet, 'Or perhaps they *are* cavorting with the natives after all?' at which, he threw the booklet on the table in front of me. Ted cowered into his bed, so I reached down to stroke his head and reassure him that he didn't need to be worried.

I adjusted the angle of my head in order to see the writing on the cover of the booklet. It was an instruction manual for men in the forces which told them how to remain healthy while serving overseas. Jack had read it while he was waiting for his medical and was now well versed about its contents. Flicking through it I could see it covered such things as how to stop yourself from getting food poisoning, being infected by water parasites, becoming infected by each other's body fluids, one example was that they were to refrain from urinating anywhere but in the latrines. And then I saw the part of the booklet he had been referring to – the men were being reminded of the importance of chastity. I couldn't believe it – surely that was obvious, that men should remain loyal to their wives? 'You don't think the soldiers are over there having affairs, do you Jack?' At which, he just shrugged and reached past me for a piece of bread.

That night neither of us slept. We sat up all night talking about what we would do once this war was over. We talked about how we would take Florence to the seaside, go on a trip to London, or perhaps we could save really hard and go to Paris, or even Canada? We could take her to see her Uncle Henry, her new Aunt Maisie, and her cousin Mary?

As the dawn broke, Jack reached for his shirt and pulled on his breeches. I couldn't believe this would be the last time I would see him for a long while – I imagined not until the war ended, whenever that might be.

I watched him as he walked away from me. Florence was in my arms clinging to me, and little Ted was scurrying around our feet, utterly oblivious to all that was going on around him. As long as he had Florence to play with, he wasn't bothered about anything else. He was her protector; her friend. When Jack reached the corner of the street he turned around and called out 'I'll write as soon as I can, Grace, I love you.' A couple of young schoolboys walked past and sniggered at Jack's open expression of devotion. Jack tutted at them, laughed, and then turned and waved back to me.

And with that, he was gone.

I thought about going to see the authorities; to tell them they had got it all wrong, that my Jack couldn't go to fight because he was a very sick man. I thought about revealing all to them about the convulsions he sometimes had in the middle of the night. If they knew about them then he would have to come home, but the more I planned to do it, the more I talked myself out of it. It wasn't my place to do that – they would find out soon enough that all wasn't quite right with him, and he would be back on the next boat home. I was sure of it.

The gaps in industry left by the men leaving the city meant that women had to return to work. Where before the war all the married women I knew were completely dependent on their husbands for money, suddenly they had their own – it was less than the men had been paid for doing the same job, but nevertheless, it was money they would not have had before. Because Florence was still very young, I didn't work, but it was difficult just having to rely on the money we received from Jack's army wages. Some families I knew flourished and some, like my father, financially anyway, were better off than they had been before the war, but many were destitute and desperate for money to buy food to feed their family. The war had become a part of everyone's life, and just as the government had intended when they wrote the guidelines for defending the realm, we were all in it together – working as one united team.

Where people could help each other, they did, and families in particular, what remained of them anyway, had to pull together to assist one another. With Father having the public house he had many contacts, and we were luckier than most in that as the war progressed we didn't go hungry. As part of those Defence of the Realm Arrangements enforced by the government, the beer Father sold had to be watered down to make it go further. Father was horrified at this, but he had to comply. Not many complained to him about the watered down taste of his beer – they didn't dare in case he barred them from entering his pub – the sergeant's attitude of the Boer War had never left him.

My cooking and baking skills have always been something which have left a lot to be desired, to the extent that Jack was always incredibly polite about the food I placed in front of him, and hence, Mr. Curtis was someone I continued to depend on for my supply of bread. I used to wrap Florence up cosy and warm, and the two of us would walk Ted to his shop so we could all stand and inhale that beautiful scent of freshly baked bread. Our loss of Adeline was always on my mind, and visiting the shop reminded me of a time when I still had her safe inside my belly; a time before she entered this cruel world; a time when we were still a family. Mr. Curtis had been devastated when he discovered Adeline had died – he said that her death just about summed up the horrendous atrocities that were going on in the world. He said my poor, innocent dead baby was a symbol of the injustice that was affecting working class families. I wasn't really sure what he meant by that, and I think in his own way he was trying to make me feel better. He didn't, but I appreciated that he cared about what had happened.

Edwin, our 'boy' soldier, had been away for almost two years. He had had leave, but had not managed to get home. He frequently wrote home to Edwin Senior and Mary-Ann, and they were always in good spirits whenever his letters arrived. They used to read them out loud to me, and it seemed as though he was bearing up. Although his letters were upbeat, there were times when I felt he was staying positive for Mary-Ann's sake. There was often more that was left unsaid which felt more poignant than what he actually did say. Because Edwin was her only boy away fighting the war who wasn't married, or who didn't have a sweetheart, as in Alfred's case, all of Edwin's letters went to Mary-Ann; there was no dilution of what he was saying, as he was communicating it all to his parents through these letters, and I picked up on the occasional sadness, fear and homesickness that Mary-Ann didn't, or chose not to. He would enthuse about his longing for the smell of Mary-Ann's wonderful cooking and the joy of us all gathering around the piano, George expertly playing tunes on those black and white keys, and the rest of us singing. He said the weather had been fine – quite hot some days, and he mused about there being an end to this war soon? As though it were a question we all could answer. He asked us whether the leaders of the world who were involved in this conflict would realise once the war had been raging on for two years that this was enough; that they had to look inside their hearts and put an end to it.

Meanwhile, Jack got in touch with me often, and while his letters, too, were upbeat, unlike Edwin's letters to their mother, there were times when he worried me because he was almost *too* graphic about what he was experiencing. He told me he was in a place called Salonica. I had never heard of it and had to go to the library in town to find a book that would tell me where it was: I discovered it was a part of Greece – right on the coast. When I looked at the map the librarian had laid out on the table for me, Salonica seemed so very far away; when others' husbands were based in France, at the time it seemed unfair, but when I thought about it logically, whether it was four hundred miles or four thousand, in the end it didn't matter how far away they were, it was whether they would ever come back that mattered.

Jack's regiment had arrived in Salonica as part of

reinforcements. I discovered in later years that people don't really talk about what happened in Salonica, however there were more men based there than people would ever imagine. People said it was not frontline fighting, but that it was more of a 'waiting game' in hot, almost unbearably so, conditions that were complicated by diseases such as malaria.

Malaria was something we knew nothing of here in Britain. I had vague recollections of it from when I was living abroad as a child, but suddenly it was one of the words on the lips of we Brits, alongside other words such as 'trenches' and 'bayonet'. These were words we had not needed to mention before and there we were saying them more or less on a daily basis.

I went back to the library to find out everything I could about malaria, and discovered it was caused by a tiny parasite which lives in the blood and is transmitted through bites from mosquitoes. It wasn't an infection we ever got in Britain, as it only affected those in much hotter climates. It can be very debilitating for those who are unlucky enough to be affected, causing a fever interspersed with shivering and, eventually, because it affects the red blood cells, it makes the person anaemic. It is an infection which is capable of killing those who are not so strong in the first place.

I decided to not go to the library to investigate anything else – it was far too worrying for me – some things I was probably better off not knowing about; learning about these things just made me worry all the more about what was going on in Salonica and how Jack was coping.

A railway which passed through Macedonia linked Salonica in Greece with Belgrade – the capital of Serbia. It is strange how you can go through life knowing a fair amount about the world and its peoples, and then suddenly, a place you had never heard of in your life before becomes the one place about which you want to know everything; knowledge of it becomes something integral to your whole being. Salonica became the first thing I thought about each morning and my last thought before I went to sleep. My Jack was there, so many, many miles away – and there was nothing neither he nor I could do to bring him back. The British forces were there with some of the French troops to defend the port of Salonica. In the earlier part of the war, Greece had two governments: a royalist pro-German government that was based in Athens, and a pro-British one in Salonica. In 1917, with its two governments united, Greece joined the war on the side of Britain, France, and Russia – the three countries which had become known as the 'Triple Entrente'.

Jack wrote home and I was horrified when he said he hadn't been feeling so good – he said he found the heat to be overbearing. I worried about him and tried when I wrote back to him to suggest ways in which he could keep himself cool. He never mentioned how he had been sleeping. The other men must have noticed that he wasn't quite right – that he was sick, but perhaps he covered it up. I'm not sure how he was doing that though. If the heat was as bad as he said, and I think then I hadn't understood just *how* hot it was over there (we had had hot summers in England, but nothing like it was in Greece), then he must have been having those fits he was prone to having. He must have – without a doubt in my mind he absolutely *must* have been having convulsions.

As the months rolled on, families all over the country were hearing about the loss of their loved ones, and each day I woke and dreaded the knock at the door. More and more we were hearing of men we knew who had been killed in action or were missing: Johnny in the next street – killed in action, Mr. Curtis' nephew, Albert – killed in action, my second cousin's husband – missing presumed dead. Some people were finding out their loved ones had been killed because their own letters were being returned to them with the words 'Missing presumed dead' thoughtlessly scrawled across the front, but many people found out through the delivery of a telegram. It felt as though there was some huge serpent sneaking up on us, getting ready to pounce so it could wrap itself around us and slowly squeeze out each last breath. And there was nothing any of us could do about it.

Except hope.

In the summer of 1916, as I was busy keeping the two and a half-year old Florence entertained, while simultaneously worrying about Jack's whereabouts – what he was doing and what he was finding to eat, Edwin's battalion, the Royal Warwickshires, were in France. In June, Robert, one of Edwin's old school friends who had gone with Edwin to sign up, came home – another injured victim of the war. He was missing an arm and had sustained a blow to his head, which everyone blamed for his apparent nonsensical talk. He spoke of guns, shrapnel, the tanks, the rats, the cold they had experienced in winter, the almost waist-high mud, and the long, long nights. They were incessant ramblings and his mother tried to make sense of what he was saying to her, but it was difficult.

As time went by, Robert became more coherent and was able to tell of life in the trenches, and how it had been for him and Edwin. He said that Edwin was being brave and reassured Mary-Ann that he was finding enough to eat. In Christmas 1914 they had stayed in a little village in the north of France. The Mayor of Birmingham had made sure that each of the men in the regiment had received a Christmas dinner

– Christmas pudding and all. They had also been given a bottle of beer to enjoy – a touch of Yuletide joy given in gratitude to these brave, British soldiers.

Robert told us they had not been there long before their battalion suffered a measles outbreak and anyone who was infected had to be isolated. Some of the battalion died of the virus – as if the war wasn't enough for them to contend with? Robert laughed, though, as he recalled that because both he and Edwin had been infected – this meant they and many others from their regiment were placed away from the other troops in a chateau with pretty nurses looking after them and, he went on, 'the coughing, the runny eyes, sneezing and runny nose, the fever, and that awful rash, they were nothing compared to what we were having to face on The Front.'

Sometimes the men received chocolate in their food parcels from the ladies of Cadbury. The men were delighted to have received a small piece of home; yet how it made them long for the comforts they had taken for granted in the years preceding the war. Whether those pre-war home comforts would have included 1lb bars of chocolate I doubt, though, as I'm sure the majority of the soldiers who went to fight in the trenches would have been unable to have afforded such food items. George and Edwin certainly hadn't been able to, and Robert said that while some men very quickly devoured theirs, Edwin had carefully divided his into small squares – rationing it to make it last, and squirreling it away where no one would find it. And then, each time he wanted a piece, he leaned back and closed his eyes, then he would carefully place it on his tongue and suck it slowly, allowing its essence of homeliness to fill his senses. On one occasion, Robert had asked him why he did that, and he told him it was because, for just those few minutes he was back in his mother's kitchen watching her bake, and listening to the kettle whistling as it steamed away on the top of the stove; those moments of home kept him sane.

Once they had recovered from the measles virus, they had to take turns at manning and patrolling The Front, and Robert said they tried to keep positive but that they were constantly watching over their shoulders, their guard never down. There was a sense that all we were hearing from The Front – in the news and in letters we received – was a stark contrast to the stories we heard from those who had been there and experienced what was happening. We began to feel that perhaps we were being naive, but now when I look back at all that happened, it is much easier for me to see that naivety was a sign of the time.

In June 1916, the War Office made an official statement about the government's position regarding under-age soldiers. They declared that those under seventeen were to be immediately discharged from service and any over seventeen, but under the age of nineteen, were to be placed in the reserve. As Edwin was born in 1896, by this point he was nineteen and a half, and he therefore had to remain on the Western Front for the foreseeable future. Entering the war as not much more than a boy, he had grown up during his time fighting and now, at nineteen, was finally considered to be a man. Mary-Ann was distraught, but there was nothing that could be done. Some local boys who had tried to foil the system, returned. Some of them were as young as fourteen – how they had got away with it I'll never understand.

The Battle of the Somme became one of the major battles, probably the best known battle, of those that happened in the war. This particular battle lasted from 1st July 1916 until 13th November of the same year. By the time Edwin's Battalion arrived in the area there had already been catastrophic losses of life on both sides, including, on the first day of battle, twenty thousand Allied losses of life. Many of those marching towards the Somme region will have known of these losses, but gradually, Edwin's battalion made their way there and, on 19th July 1916, they took over an area near High Wood, with the intention of taking a farm track known as Wood Lane, and attacked through the night of July 22nd and into the morning of the 23rd. Edwin's battalion, the Royal 14th/1st Warwickshires had gone 'over the top' to face the enemy. *Over the top* – such a strange expression, which we've lately come to use so flippantly, but for the men in those trenches, it was a matter of life or death, not an expression of someone's over-excitement or over dramatisation of something.

An incident happened during the fighting that night involving a tree which had been noticed by one of the sergeants. There was a solitary tree situated on the Allies' side of the front line and this particular sergeant was wounded early on in the fighting. In the distance he saw the lone tree and started crawling towards it for shelter. On his way he gathered a group of wounded men. That single tree, on that night, was probably responsible for saving the lives of those men.

Forty men died in that battle, while two hundred were missing in action, believed to be dead.

While we all slept safely in our beds, we were unaware of the fact that within a few days we would learn that one of those who died on that night was our dear Edwin Junior – our own 'boy soldier'. He was nineteen years old; just nineteen.

A long time after the war, sometime in the 1930s, and having a renewed, almost insatiable, thirst for information, I discovered a book in the library that had been written by the Lieutenant-Colonel of

Edwin's regiment and I copied a passage out of it to give to Mary-Ann and Edwin Senior (it's funny how we all carried on calling him that even after Edwin Junior had died, I suppose we wanted to continue to acknowledge that Edwin had been such a big part of our lives). The passage was about the night that Edwin died:

"It is comforting to remember that the companies went to the charge in magnificent style, never faltering or hesitating, in face of a murderous fire, and Birmingham has reason to be proud of her sons and of the courage they displayed in the face of hopeless odds."

Mary-Ann kept the piece of paper I gave her until the day she died – I found it in a wooden box next to her bed when we were clearing out her house.

After Edwin's death the whole family entered a period of desperate mourning. He had been so very young and we could not comprehend why he had been taken from us. We all sat around shaking our heads and wondering out loud, 'Why, oh why?' But no one was able to answer and the silence became a deafening throb that echoed in our bosoms.

We held a service in the church and invited Edwin's friends' families to come back to the house afterwards. Edwin's friend Robert was there with his family. It was like a funeral, but there was no body; a wake with no sense of closure. Mary-Ann was inconsolable – her neck was bent forwards and her shoulders shook uncontrollably as she sat in the front pew of the church flanked by Edwin Senior and their daughter Beck. Her youngest boy Frank held tightly to his father's arm. 'My boy, my sweet, sweet boy,' Mary-Ann repeated over and over again. Her words were interspersed with incomprehensible sounds which were like the beginnings of some heartbreaking primeval wail. There was nothing any of us could do to console her; what could we possibly have said or done? Absolutely nothing could repair her loss. They say time heals, but time simply stores the grief in a compartment of the brain which is periodically opened when a person is alone and all the missing and longing come tumbling out; society can't cope with outward signs of grief so they are secreted away.

I was seated in the second row of hardwood benches, with Alfred's now-fiancée Ellen, Agnes and the girls. I had Florence nestled close to my side, while my father and Florrie, Tom and Leah were in the pew behind us. As the minister finished the sermon with The Lord's Prayer, I reached out to Florence and hugged her closer to me. *'Please don't let them take her daddy away from her,'* I prayed so no one would hear.

When the organ began its woeful tune, indicating our time was up – we could leave and take all our grief with us, Father reached forward and touched the back of my head and stroked my hair. With tears streaming down my face, I turned and caught his eye. His normally brusque demeanour was broken; he, too, was suffering in this war. Maybe it was because he couldn't control what was happening – he knew that Bill was in India, but that was it, he had no knowledge about his true whereabouts. Everything that happened to him was in the lap of the gods; just as it was for George, Alfred, and my dear Jack.

As we walked out of the church I glanced at Robert. He had the strangest expression. In my mind I can still see his face now, and I wonder what he was thinking. His face was white and his jaw was set in a hard line. His eyes were distant and he looked at me, but his expression did not change. It was as though he was looking right through me. I felt a shiver pass down my spine.

Two months later, Robert killed himself with some strychnine he had found in his father's outbuildings. He had survived his war, but the war had taken him anyway.

Chapter 5

The Relentless War

After Edwin's death we all knew that nothing would ever be the same again. Before there had been hope that our family would be reunited, but now there was this giant, gaping, aching hole. How could there ever be another family event, another hot summer's day or frost-laden wintry morning when we wouldn't think of them; wouldn't go to mention their name, but then stop ourselves lest we upset someone else in the family? To constantly remind ourselves that they had been a part of our lives – was that what everyone wanted? Did they want us to talk about the dead, to include their names in our conversations? Or were we to simply remain quiet and behave as though nothing had happened – as though they had never existed, and their time here on earth had become void? It is a strange thing, death, and with each soldier who died it was difficult to know how each next of kin they had left behind would want the rest of us to behave.

Edwin had been Mary-Ann's favourite – her baby for six years, and he had seen her through one of the toughest times of her life when her daughter Emily died – her little girl who died at the age of just three in 1901. Everyone said that she bestowed all her love on Edwin when that happened – when little Frank came along two years later, she didn't seem able to give him the same affection she had given Emily. She had loved and lost three babies and was living in desperate fear of losing another. At six, Edwin had passed the dangerous stage, so he was the one – always the one.

A letter arrived from Canada from Henry's new wife to say that Henry had left for France as one of the many men and women who had signed up to go and support the war effort. Once more, Mary-Ann was to cope with one of her sons being involved in the bitter conflict.

As Christmas 1916 drew nearer, she had something to keep her occupied because Alfred returned home for a short time. He and Ellen suddenly announced that they were getting married – their engagement was not going to wait until after the war after all. 'What is the sense in waiting?' they said, almost simultaneously.

'This war may *never* end.' Ellen added, with a look of resentment passing over her perfect face with its fine, almost ornamental, features. Her comment was met with stunned silence by all who were there that day, but she simply shrugged her shoulders and tossed her dark curls.

The thought that the war might never end certainly never entered my mind. What if it didn't? Could there really be a war in which a truce was never drawn? A victory never claimed? No end which could lead to a new beginning?

Alfred had managed to get recovery leave for two weeks because he had been hit by a shell. He had a deep flesh wound on his thigh which the doctors had managed to suture, but it was taking a while to heal. He asked if he could recover back in Blighty rather than in the army hospital and they had granted this leave to him – telling him they would be glad of the hospital space.

At last he was able to marry his sweetheart, and not only that, he would be home with his family for Christmas. There was only a short time to prepare for the wedding: Ellen, luckily, had made her wedding dress in advance of him being granted leave. She, too, had to get special leave from the munitions factory, and was due back at the factory on Boxing Day – the war would stop for no one. Their wedding was set for Christmas Eve, mine and Jack's fifth anniversary, and I found that difficult, but I had to put my own feelings aside and get on with celebrating this wonderful, happy event with these two beautiful young people.

Ellen was a gorgeous bride. She had a flair and natural beauty which made women envy her. Through working in the munitions factory she had made a lot of friends – many of whom lined the pews at the church that day. As she walked down the aisle with her father, the few men who were there gasped, while the women secretly seethed at the exquisiteness of

89

this gorgeous creature.

Alfred was equally taken aback when he caught sight
of his bride, and the look of complete joy on his face
is one of the few images of wartime I like to
remember. For that one day, while the celebrations
continued, we could forget what was happening on
foreign shores and allow ourselves a little freedom
from the worries that had enshrouded our lives.

Christmas with one of the boys home was the most
beautiful gift we could have had – we all had to
remind ourselves that these newly-weds would want
time to themselves, but each time Alfred sat down at
a table to eat or sat chatting to his father, there were
three young ladies demanding his attention –
Florence, and Agnes' two daughters, who sat around
him in a semi-circle – hanging on to his every word
and staring at him as though they had never seen
anything quite like him before. This young, handsome
man became their idol for the few short days he was
home with us. We didn't need to entertain those girls,
they were quite, quite happy with the entertainment
they had discovered for themselves.

Alfred, in turn, was completely absorbed by the
children, and Ellen, in the end, had to admit defeat.
Her time with him could only be once the children
had all had their piece of him, and when his mother
had hugged him a thousand times – just to make sure
he was really there with her. At one point I walked

into the front room with Ellen and the two of us laughed as we saw Alfred in the centre of the settee, with Florence sat on his lap, Agnes' girls one either side of him, and Frank sat directly in front of him on a kitchen chair with his legs splayed over the seat and the back of the chair facing towards Alfred. Frank was cradling his head in both hands as he listened to the stories of foreign lands; holding onto Alfred's every word, just as though he were interrogating him.

By now, Frank was fourteen – a young man himself, and it seemed that never a day went by when Mary-Ann didn't mention the atrocities of war and that she had already lost one son – she constantly reminded Frank that he shouldn't even think of trying to fool the authorities and going off to try and sign up.

Before Alfred left for the Front again, I took my brothers, Tom and Sam, and my younger sister, Leah, over with me to see Alfred and Ellen, who were now both staying temporarily with Jack's parents while they tried to sort out a house to rent. We women were in the kitchen preparing our usual wartime diet of the occasional egg or two, depending on whether or not the hens we kept in the back garden were choosing to lay; some potatoes and onions we had grown in the summer and autumn and managed to effectively store in the outhouse, and anything else we had managed to procure from my father.

Thomas, Sam and Leah had arrived with a sponge

fruit cake Leah had made – even in these harsh times, Father had been able to keep a handle on people and get what he wanted from them. I don't think that people were terrified of him. I wouldn't like to think he was that frightening a man. He had just been affected by all he had done during his own service for Queen (and then King) and Country. They were harsh times, and most people were suffering, but I think that actually, and I hate to say this about him, my father was thriving. He just had ways and means of doing things, of acquiring what he wanted, and it seemed to be working for him. I saw other families struggling much more than ours was, and I felt guilty; I was a little embarrassed about it really.

After we had all eaten that night, Mary-Ann went off to bed, and the girls all lay sleeping on the rug in front of the fire, lined up side by side, arms sprawled in different directions; oblivious to the increasing tension in the room; the surge of anticipatory adrenaline coursing its way through our veins. Finally, the real questions everyone had wanted to know the answers to began to pour out of our mouths. Alfred had knowledge tucked inside his head – he was going back to The Front in just two days' time and all of us wanted to know what it was like. Were the stories true? All we had heard from others who had returned – were those stories really typical of what was going on?

Alfred confirmed pretty much everything we had heard about the awful time the men were having in the trenches – he also said, looking directly over at me with an expression on his face I found difficult to fathom, that from what they were hearing, the troops who had gone over to Salonica where Jack was, they were not really fighting as such – in fact there was not much happening at all. He said that many of them were envious that they themselves had not been posted to Greece, ' "...*an easy time of it*," is what they're saying,' he said.

I didn't know what he meant by that – was he trying to make me feel better so I wouldn't worry so much? Or did he think that Jack really *was* having an easy time of it, and he resented that? This war was so confusing, so full of contradictions. I wanted to wake Florence and bundle her and Ted up and take them home with me but, instead, I sat there listening but not taking in the rest of the conversation, unsure what to think, but trying to comprehend what was going on, and why Jack was so far away from me when apparently there was nothing going on in Greece. In the end, I decided there must be something keeping the men there, otherwise they would have brought them back west and sent them to France.

It was getting late, and we had all decided to make ourselves as comfortable as possible and stay the night. Edwin Senior brought more blankets down for

Agnes, Leah, and me so we could sleep in the same room as the girls, and Tom and Sam went to sleep in the spare room. Ted had found himself a comfortable place wedged in behind the bend of Florence's legs. He let out a deep sigh, as dogs are often prone, and nestled deeper into her warmth, making us all long for the comfort and contentment of this little dog's life.

Before the night ended, though, Alfred had one more thing he wanted to share with us. It was a thought which had come to him while he had been on duty in the trenches, rather than something that had actually happened. His face grew very serious and he told us, 'It's not like a society of modern people over there, it is as though we have been reduced to something we were hundreds of years ago – like people we have read about who lived in Mediaeval times – something akin to savages – in the ways in which we're dealing with other people.'

As we all sat listening to him, our attention on his every word, he continued, 'I once read about a man called Darwin in the newspaper. He did all these studies in the mid 1800s on animals and humans, and explained how we came to be the way we are. He talked about how the animals that survived were the fittest ones. The more I see out there, the more I think he is right. It is not necessarily those who are fittest in body who are surviving, though, but the ones who are the most cunning.' I had a flash of my father's face cross my mind and couldn't help but nod in agreement. Once he had scanned all our faces to make sure we were all paying attention, he continued once more,' they're the ones who are beating this thing, the ones who are shrewd…'

A heavy silence fell across the room as we all attempted to understand the implications of what he was saying, and in the end we didn't say much more that night – or even when the morning came. He had given us plenty to think about, and we were left to wonder about the survival behaviour of men in war.

When Alfred went back to The Front, I wondered whether *he* was one of the clever ones, and because he had recognised this as being a quality of those who were surviving, would *he* be one of the survivors? I spent many days pondering over that; sometimes that was all we had, time to ponder while we waited. I also wondered whether my Jack was one of the ones who would survive through cunning and, I suppose, strategy. Was Jack a man like that? Was he shrewd? Somehow I doubted that very much, and that thought sent shivers down my spine.

As the war charged on, I held out for the days when I would receive letters from Salonica. I needed constant affirmation that Jack was alive. He sent me floral embroidered cards with short notes neatly folded and inserted inside their flaps. On my birthday and other special occasions he sent particularly long letters, but

I was eager for news, and there was never enough.

I spent a lot of time with Agnes and the girls and we would swap notes and try to piece together what was happening in each other's husband's wars. We felt that if we talked about them over and over again we would be able to fill in the gaps, and somehow form a fuller picture of what on earth was going on which meant that we could not have our husbands here at home with us.

On 6th April 1917, the United States of America joined the war effort on the side of the Allies. As news filtered through to the troops, there must have been hope in the trenches that the war would soon be over – that is certainly how we felt back home. How could the enemy compete with a force as great as America? When I got together with Agnes on that day and we read the newspaper I had bought, we scrutinised it for clues that the war would be over soon. Any tiny intimation in things that we read or heard about having America on our side, and that this would give us the power to end the war, was taken by us to mean that, certainly by the summer anyway, we would have Jack, George, and the rest of our men home.

We couldn't have been more wrong! How could we have known then that the war was to rumble on for another year and a half? I think that if we had known that at that point, then many of us would have given up hope of ever seeing our loved ones again.

But Agnes had a surprise when, one day in May 1917, as she was hanging the washing on the line, George appeared at the end of the entry which separated their house from the terraced house next door. He had been granted leave and, taking into account his travelling, would be home for just under four days.

He had sent a letter in advance of his leave, but she did not receive it until a week later. The girls were cautiously excited about his return, but within a day they remembered how to be with him. For children it seemed that sometimes it was easier to adapt to our changing world and its surprises. Despite having lost weight, George appeared to be coping well with the war and, in Edwin Senior and Mary-Ann's front room, we gathered around and sang songs – George playing the piano in his old familiar way.

Before long, he had gone back to France, and Agnes longed for his return, just as I longed to see my Jack back by my side.

Our food supplies were running very short by now and extreme rationing had begun. Much of the grain we needed was coming in from America, and some of the boats had been sunk in the Atlantic by enemy submarines. By early spring, most of the food we had grown the previous year and managed to preserve in jars, bottle, or carefully store in the outhouses, had gone; our new seeds and potatoes had been planted, but were not even showing through the ground yet.

For the first time in all the war even Father was beginning to look worried, and that worried me – he was our back-up. He was the one we ran to when we were in need of something other than what we could grow or buy ourselves. Mr. Curtis was still offering extras to Florence and me whenever we bought food from him. He had expanded his range as the bakery was no longer able to sustain itself. Because he had such a large garden behind the shop, he had managed to grow a lot of food – far more than he and Mrs. Curtis could manage to eat, and he had many varieties of homemade preserves on display in the shop, although, because sugar was in demand due to it being something we had to import, I have to admit that much of it was quite sour.

Without warning, my brother Tom went to go and do his 'bit' for the war. Like Edwin had been when he signed up back in 1914, he, too, was just 17 and must have lied about his age. Was there nothing I had ever told him which would have made him understand that perhaps he should have stayed at home for as long as he legally could? Bill was already away in India, and I suppose with our military upbringing it was natural for them – almost inevitable – that they would follow in Father's footsteps. Bill had no choice but to go, but at that point Tom did – he could have stayed at home where he was safe. I had stopped trying to understand why anyone would choose to go and fight when they didn't have to, especially when we all knew what had happened to poor Edwin.

George and Alfred wrote regularly to Agnes and Ellen. They were both remaining positive about everything in their letters, but then, as we had already realized, you could never tell with the letters whether what was being said was truth, or what was being said to placate those of us who were left behind.

We tried to stop Tom from going, but there was something in him, something which told us that this was what he wanted, and nothing on this earth was going to stop him. Father simply became silent – as he got older and as the war progressed, I think that even *he* became sick of what was going on. There was no reward, no gratitude, no escape, and no finality – except in death.

Determined, though, Tom went off and signed up to be with the Welsh Fusiliers. Before long, we heard he was with the Gurkhas in India, close to the Himalayan Mountains. Within weeks, however, Father got a message to say Tom was ill – he had double pneumonia, and the doctor at the military camp had told him he would not live to see his eighteenth birthday. We prepared ourselves to lose him. He was just seventeen for Heaven's sake – how could this cruel, cruel war continue taking and taking?

Weeks passed and we heard nothing of his progress, but then a miracle happened – amid this dark, dark war, there was a glimmer of hope – my dear brother, Tom, his young body was strong; he fought back and recovered from his illness. His diseased lungs had healed.

Florence was four years old by that time, and in the darkest hours of one cold, cold December night, I awoke with a start because Ted was barking and scratching at the kitchen door downstairs. I called out to him to be quiet, which he did, but then I could hear a rhythmic groan emanating from Florence's room. The house was cold and I had tucked her tightly under her bed covers to keep her warm. On opening the door, I could immediately see that she'd kicked her blankets away from her and was tossing and turning with a fever.

Suddenly not aware of the freezing cold night, I raced downstairs, grasped some towels, and soaked them in the coldest of water. With Ted frantically dancing around my heels, I charged upstairs and placed the towels around Florence to cool her fevered body and hot, burning skin. Her forehead exuded beads of sweat and I carefully placed a cold cloth across her forehead, talking to her, but all the time fearful that she was slipping away from me.

In the days that followed she slipped in and out of consciousness, and each time she began to come round I thought I had managed to save her and that my sweet, beautiful little girl was going to be okay.

Father paid for a doctor to come out to visit and he said she had the flu. I knew that, and I wanted to know what to do with her – how I could make her better. With a glance to my father, and then back to me, he said tentatively, 'Just carry on with what you're doing – that's all you can do.' He then added, quite brutally I felt at the time, 'She'll either live or she won't. That's the way it is.' And, with a helpless shrug, he was gone.

His flippant way of dealing with me had strengthened my resolve to save her. Whatever I did well in this life, the one thing I would absolutely succeed with was to save my daughter. If there was something the doctor's insensitivity had served, it was to make me more even more determined.

I thought that God was punishing me for Tom having survived from his illness. In the scheme of things, I felt that someone had created a rule which said that I could only get to keep one of them and all my prayers had been for Tom, so he was the one I would get to keep.

I did deals with the supernatural forces I had been pleading with since the war had started. I promised to be good and never have bad thoughts about anyone – to be kind and gentle with everyone on this earth for the rest of my life. I even told this force to take me instead, but no force answered me – there were no signs: no crashing of thunder or banging of drums, no sparks of light emanating from the sky. Just me and Florence – she prostrate in a feverish wait for death, and me by her side, waiting.

But then, amazingly, slowly, gradually, over the coming days she came back from those gates of death, and I had my baby back. I gave her a sip of whisky Father had given me to try, and there was a flicker of life as she let out a noise which sounded as though she was calling me. And then she opened her eyes.

She was weak, but she had come back to me – somehow we had beaten the odds, and I got to keep her as well as my brother.

Chapter 6

December 1917 – 1918

I lost all communication with Jack. It had been a month or more since I had last heard from him. I feared the worst – every one of us feared the worst. How could someone you love be so far away in a country torn apart by war and you not worry?

Through his regular letters to me I had kept his family up-to-date with how he was, and they had noticed the sudden dearth of news. When Florence was sick I wrote to him so he would know, but there was no reply. I was sure that had he been okay, he would have replied, so I wrote again, and again, and again.

Over many weeks I wrote every day, and then waited quietly, watching for the post for news from him. When I saw there was no post, my heart sank, but the longer no word from him continued, the more I dreaded my own letters being returned with a message saying he had been killed. Eventually, just before Christmas 1917, I wrote to his force in Salonica asking what had happened to him. I figured that if I wrote directly to his regiment telling them that I was certain there must be something wrong with him, that he must be in hospital… or otherwise… then they would be certain to let me know how he was. I couldn't bear to suggest to them that he might be dead. By saying it, it might have tempted fate, and if he wasn't dead already, then fate, or whatever force it was which dictated who lived and who died, may just decide that that was the way it was going to be.

Despite my desperate letter to the regiment, there was still no news. I knew they were busy with their war and everything, but I needed to know if my Jack was okay! Christmas came and went. Neither my family nor Jack's felt like celebrating. We had had enough. We felt cheated by the government; by our country.

We wanted our boys back home.

Finally, in January 1918, I received a letter from the Royal Garrison Artillery (RGA) Office in Dover. I still have that letter tucked away in the wooden box in my bedroom. My hands were shaking as I carefully opened that letter. The relief that flooded through me when I read its words is indescribable. They were reassuring me that, at that point anyway, 'no notification of any casualty to this soldier has so far been received'. It went on to say that 'so far as this office is aware, he is well.'

The reality of war is such that soldiers sometimes do not return, and my choice of words when I had written to Jack's regiment and said 'or otherwise…' well, I suppose I was forcing them into communicating with me. I was desperate, and this letter from them brought me hope. It went on to inform me that should any casualty be reported in relation to 'Gunner Cogbill', the family would be immediately informed. That made me feel bad – when I had been so desperate to find him, I hadn't given a thought to those whose loved ones HAD been injured or killed. That's probably why the regiment had been so slow in responding. I suppose they had other things to occupy their time…telling someone their husband or son had died was more important than letting some fraught, anxious, seemingly-obsessive woman know that there was nothing wrong with her husband.

Just a few weeks later, however, it transpired that Jack *had* been in hospital at the time I had received the letter from his regiment because, in February, he finally came home to Britain. This slight (he was just five feet seven inches tall and not what you would ever call well-built or muscular), vulnerable man of mine had experienced great difficulty during the thirteen months he was based in Greece until, finally, following him having suffered from repeated periods of epilepsy and hysteria, on 5th February 1918, he got his wish and was allowed to return to Birmingham.

He arrived at the General Hospital in Edgbaston on 21st February 1918, where it was recommended he be discharged from active service, but before they could do that, they needed to try to treat him – not physically though, there was nothing obvious with him that you could see, but psychologically he was in a state.

He had been ill in Salonica for several weeks, and as soon as they were able to move him they had taken him back to the military hospital so that doctors could assess his condition. I had *known* there had been something wrong with him. In my heart, I had been sure there was something. Maybe there is some link which enables you to communicate with one another across the miles? Perhaps from his hospital bed thousands of miles away there had been something which bound us together? Was there a message that reached me from him while he was lying there unconscious? Is there something like that? I don't know. I imagine no one can know for sure, but as he lay there I was convinced there had been something wrong, and that was why I had been so desperate to find out how he was.

Once he was back in Birmingham and I was allowed to visit him, immediately I saw him in that clinical ward, lying on the starched white sheets of the hospital bed, I knew.

This was *not* my Jack.

This was a man *like* Jack – he looked like him, and his voice sounded the same as he used to, but I knew straight away that the Jack I had known had been left on the battlefields of Salonica. There was absentness in his gaze. He appeared to recognise me and he smiled, but the smile was apprehensive and distant; the corners of his mouth were turned up, but his eyes did not reflect any hint of that smile.

Optimistically hoping that seeing Florence might help him in his recovery, I took her to the hospital to see this man she had never really known – he was even more of a stranger to her than he was to me. It was difficult for me to comprehend how I should feel. The man I had missed so much for those two years had disappeared, and I tried to understand what he had gone through, and how it had made him like he now was, but I couldn't. His experiences of the war had somehow penetrated his mind in a way which had made him no longer remember the family he had left behind.

Florence knew her daddy was back and that he was poorly, however, in no way did that prepare her for seeing him. I realised very quickly I had made a mistake in taking her to visit him when we walked through the door to the ward, and I could see he was surrounded by hospital staff who were pinning him to the bed trying to give him an injection to calm him down. A nurse who was brandishing a syringe glanced up and acknowledged me, but then I saw a look of panic flash across her face when she noticed Florence by my side. A rush of adrenaline tore my feet away from where I had become rooted to the floor and, without further hesitation, I picked Florence up and dashed through the doors of the hospital into the freezing morning air.

We navigated our way as quickly as we could across the ice-laden pathways; away, far, far away from the stark white walls and the troubled, dribbling, trembling, star-gazing men who rocked backwards and forwards in their beds, reliving their nightmares and calling out in their sleep to the comrades they'd lost on the battlefield.

Medical staff reassured me that Jack would improve as time went by, and that I would be able to have him home soon. A doctor told me that being at home in familiar surroundings would help Jack's recovery. When he said that, it frightened me and, I have to admit, I no longer wanted him home. I was frightened for myself, but even more frightened for Florence. I had seen the way Jack flew into a rage when the hospital staff tried to give him his medication; fighting them off and screeching inhuman sounds. I didn't know quite how I would cope if he did that when he came home. What would I say to the little Florence who was now just over four years old? How would I explain that this man, this lovely man who had turned into some kind of monster, was the father whose picture I had repeatedly shown her and said, 'This is your sweet, wonderful daddy, Florence, and one day he will come home to us'?

Not wanting to expose Florence to any more traumatic hospital visits, Mary-Ann took care of her for me while I went each day to spend a couple of hours at Jack's bedside. It was a freezing cold February and I was glad of the cream knitted hat, scarf and gloves my sister, Leah, had made for me at Christmas time. Jack was on a ward with other men who had come back from the war, and each of them was clearly experiencing similar psychological problems to him – only all to varying degrees. In addition to their psychological scars, some of them had physical wounds and, just like our neighbour, poor Arthur, some had amputations. It was not a place for a little girl to be.

In between episodes of rage, Jack had periods of quiescence during which he would lie on his side and hold tightly to my hand, delivering short bursts of information about what he had experienced in Salonica. It transpired that, in 1917, in the first summer after he left Birmingham, Jack had experienced seizures while on duty in the hot, Greek sun. His regiment was involved in heavy fighting on the Doiran Front in Salonica. The battle continued over a few months, although they made no dent in the enemy's defences. He said all the men thought it was pointless.

At one point, when the heat would have been overbearing for anyone, but for someone who was prone to epilepsy it must have been unbearable, Jack went down into a fit at the side of the road. I could remember the heat of my childhood in India and Africa, and knew some of what he must have gone through. Memories of hazy, sunshine days, when the only place to be comfortable was in the whitewashed buildings, padding about on cold stone floors, came back to me, but in Greece there had been nowhere for Jack to hide from the sun.

He told me he had been hospitalised after that occasion, but that the seizures were happening far more often than anyone realised, and when he finished up in hospital after the event by the side of the road, because he remained without fits for the next few days, he got the impression that no one believed that he was ill – that he was putting it on to try to get home. 'Can you believe that, Grace'?' he asked me, not expecting me to answer him, 'They actually thought I would fabricate something like that.' And with that, he tutted, and shook his head in disbelief.

Surrounded by bars to stop him from falling off the

bed, he leaned across them, looked directly into my eyes, and recalled what had happened. He had received a scrape on his head from a shell injury – a near miss – about a year before, and had been hospitalised. It had been since then that his fits had become much worse.

On one particular day he had gone down quite suddenly with a fit, and was found convulsing at the side of the road by some of the other men. What he told me was quite coherent, and I began to hope he was getting better. He went on to say, 'The scratch from the shell – it was like something had exploded deep inside my brain.' With this, he reached up and touched the left side of his head.

He went on, 'I couldn't hear, couldn't see. I thought I had had it, Grace. I thought I was gone. I thought I would never see you again.' He began to sob, and I held his hand tightly, waiting for him to compose himself – hoping he would be able to.

Eventually, he began to speak again, 'All around me there was smoke from gunfire and dust, so, so much dust, and I crouched down and held my head. It throbbed and throbbed. Something was pounding inside my skull, and no longer able to bear my weight I fell to the ground, gasping for breath and writhing in pain. Lying there in No Man's Land, I could sense that men were rushing past me, and I could smell the stench of dust and the sickly but sweet smell of blood. I began to submit to it, to let myself became absorbed by what I thought was death; to let it enshroud my body and steal my soul. But then, suddenly, I felt someone grab hold of my collar, and then another grasped my arm and clutched hold of the back of my belt – I was being dragged over the rough, Greek terrain. In the distance I heard faint words as though someone was whispering my name. 'Jack, Jack, you're okay, Jack. We'll get you back,' they told me. I opened my eyes to see where the voices were coming from, but I could see only blackness.'

While Jack held tightly to my hand, I found myself wanting nothing more than to let go and run away; to retreat to the time when we were young and everything was light and wonderful. This, whatever it was, this charade, was not what we had expected our lives would be like. Unable to tear myself away from his grip, I forced myself to reach forward with my other hand to stroke the side of his dark, wavy hair.

Familiarity oozed through the pores of my fingers – subconsciously, slowly. I began to recognise a tiny shred of what he had been. (*Jack? Is this you? Could this be you?*).

Focusing his eyes on mine once more, I looked back

at him *(those blue, blue eyes? Jack? Is that you?)*, and he continued with his story. 'Back in the trench someone put bandages around my head and I was transferred to a stretcher. They took me to the hospital tents, and three weeks I was there for, Grace. Three weeks. It took a whole week before I could see, longer for me to hear properly again, and throughout it all I was confused and I don't really remember much else about what happened.' A puzzled frown appeared between his eyes.' How could time disappear like that, Grace?'

How could I answer such a question?

As he spoke, I recalled the time he was telling me about – that time when he had been in hospital in Salonica in April 1917, I had not received any post from him for two weeks, and then an embroidered card arrived. There was no message except 'My dearest Grace, I love you, Jack' It was several weeks after that before I received a proper letter from him saying he had been injured by a shell, that he had been in hospital, but was now on the road to recovery – he was back on duty at the front line. It had been a positive letter, but reading between the lines, I had known there were things he wasn't telling me.

At the time I received that letter I remembered I had secretly wanted him to be in hospital for longer. In hospital he was safe – back on the front line he was risking his life every day. At home that spring and early summer of 1917, as I used to lie in bed under the sheets and brightly-coloured, crocheted blankets, and pull them around my head to cocoon myself, I had prayed that someone would put him safely in the hospital until the war was over. Shortly after that I had received another card from him. He had been in hospital yet again – after being sent back up the line he had collapsed once more. This time he was kept in the military hospital until he was properly better – or as better as he was going to be in that environment.

During his most recent bout of convulsions in Salonica, the bout which had resulted in him being sent home for good, one of his sergeants had witnessed him having the fit and helped him to get to the shade.

The sergeant who had witnessed Jack having the fit was instrumental in getting him brought home to Blighty. Jack told me that on his medical forms he had been asked to provide witnesses to what had happened. It made me wonder whether there really had been some feeling among his superiors that he was exaggerating the effects of his injuries so he could return home. I hoped not, but there was something bothering me about the whole shenanigan. I couldn't put my finger on it, but there was something suspicious. Jack told me his letters had been censored by senior officers. We all knew that censoring went on. In times of war, and we've seen enough of war in my lifetime, there is a need to make sure vital information doesn't get through, but then what use to the enemy is the information that can be sent by a mere gunner to his loved ones back home? The lack of information getting through was infuriating at times.

As the story of Jack's time in Salonica came pouring out, piece by frustrating, horrifying piece, my heart sank with regret that I had never told the authorities that he was ill before he had gone away. Would they have believed me? Would they have let him stay at home? But then, had he remained at home, would he have coped with being a potential recipient of the white feather, and all the scorn and resentment attached to being considered a coward? His illness was invisible to all who did not know him well, so he would have been tormented. On the face of things no one would have understood why he should not have gone to war.

Eventually, a few weeks after his return to Birmingham, on 14th March 1918, Jack was considered to be fit enough to leave the hospital and come home. He was formally discharged from the army through ill health, and the three of us attempted to reassemble our lives into some kind of ordered manner.

Making his way through the front door, it very quickly became apparent that he didn't recognise the inside of our house. It was as though he had never been inside its walls. He walked around picking up ornaments and cups and holding them up to the light in order to scrutinise their intricacies.

I settled him down in the front room and offered him a cup of tea. When I returned with his cup and saucer he was standing again. He stood directly in front of our wedding picture with his back to me. I thought he had heard me come into the room, but he clearly hadn't. At first I thought he was crying, but he stood there for what must have been several minutes, while I didn't move a single muscle. When he turned around he had the strangest expression on his face – I had expected to see tears, but he looked bewildered. There was a frown furrowing his brow and he looked at a complete loss as to who the people in the photograph were – who *we* had been, those vibrant individuals who were immortalised in the wooden frame.

Many times after that day I caught him in the same pose: staring; looking; gazing, whatever, but always with a mystified expression. I once said to him, 'Jack, just look at that, didn't we have such a wonderful day?' but he simply made an incomprehensible sound and nodded – to himself, though, not to me – and then turned away and went back to his chair.

Initially there were lots of visitors as everyone wanted to drop by to see 'Jack the War Hero'. Relatives and friends drifted in and out of the house – all with their own stories to share with Jack. Mary-Ann and Edwin Senior became an almost permanent fixture at our kitchen table – they were so relieved to have one of their sons back home safe. Mary-Ann spent virtually the entirety of each visit with her eyes fixed on Jack's face, as though she could not quite believe that he was home safe from the war at last.

For Florence and me, when there were so many people coming to see him, it was easier for us in many ways than in the times that were to come when everyone drifted away; when other men in the street became the new novelty as they returned from the war. When this happened, people flocked to their houses to visit them instead – each man was awarded temporary local fame which was a welcome distraction from the war that was still going on. I recalled Ellen's comments just before she and Alfred married, when she had said that the war might never end, and I wished with the whole of my heart that she was not right.

Florence recovered really well from the respiratory virus she had had in the December before Jack returned home, and was back to her normal self, playing happily in the back yard with Ted in the last snows of winter whenever the opportunity presented itself. These were tenuous times, however, and as if the loss of life from the four years of the war weren't enough, no sooner had Jack returned home to us, there was a massive killer on its way which would, in the end, claim even more lives than the whole of the war.

Spanish Flu, or 'La Grippe', as some people on the continent called it, was an influenza infection which swept across the world killing millions in its wake. Florence did not succumb to it. Having been ill just a short time before, I was in desperate fear that she would, but there was nothing – neither of us had a cough, not a sneeze, not a runny nose or a sore throat. Whether she had had a similar virus and the two of us had gleaned some immunity from it, I don't know, but we were both well, which helped a lot in keeping us both strong to deal with Jack and the problems he was experiencing.

Contrary to popular belief, in Europe the influenza virus did not originate in Spain, but in a place called Brest, in France, where United States troops had disembarked their boats. Initially it caused comparatively mild symptoms, and I wondered whether somehow (although I can't imagine how) Florence had caught this earlier strain of the virus, and that was what was protecting us both. I would never have said that her symptoms had been 'mild', however, as at the time I had thought she was dying.

Unlike many families, we somehow managed to avoid contracting anything that was like a full-blown version of the virus. Perhaps it *was* because at the time when Florence had caught her virus we had all developed varying degrees of something akin to flu and it was that which saved us all.

When the virus did emerge in Europe, it stuck around for about a year, eventually disappearing in 1919, almost as suddenly as it had arrived, but it left behind many more grieving families. This strain of flu claimed millions of lives across the world, even more than the war had. This 'enemy' did not distinguish between race and rank, and anyone caught up in its wake was susceptible and could die from its symptoms. The trenches became rife with it, as did the towns and villages. It stole life in plague-like proportions. The second wave of the virus was the one that killed so many people. It was an unforgiving virus. It caused all the symptoms which you would associate with 'flu', but as well as these, it caused the most terrible coughing up of blood.

It was named 'Spanish' flu because Spain had remained neutral during the conflict, and many of the earliest reported cases were from Spain. Due to its neutrality, Spanish news was not censored in the same way as everywhere else was during the war, and therefore the newspapers there were filled with reports of the disease, especially when their king became ill. Naturally, this information was being disseminated by other countries, and even though it was affecting people all over the world, it became 'Spanish'.

Many thousands of people died of it here in the United Kingdom, and everyone lived in fear of becoming infected. It presented a huge problem for our cemeteries in Birmingham, and undertakers at the local cemeteries were burying around twenty people a day. With the war and the flu, we began to wonder how the world would ever repair itself. There had been so, so much happening that we felt that something good must happen soon – either that or the whole human race would die out. The end of the war was what we all were hoping the following months would bring. Only then could anyone even attempt to rebuild their life.

There was no doubt that the success of this virus in terms of its ability to kill so many was aided by the movement of the troops and other personnel around

the world at this time; it had to have been what
helped it to spread so successfully. There is also no
doubt that the virus benefited from the poor
immunity of the population as a whole, which was
largely down to the terrible living conditions and
insufficient nutrition experienced by so many people,
especially those of the working classes. We were lucky
in that we were still being helped a lot by Father and
his ways and means of finding food. In the end, I
suppose that many of those who were weakened from
the effects of the war and lack of good food simply
did not have the ability to fight it off.

Jack gave so much of himself to the war. When he
was discharged, the war was only months away from
its Armistice. To a man already fragile from the
combination of a yet undiscovered illness, and his
apparently newly-ingrained psychological problems,
there was another devastating blow on its way when,
just three weeks after Jack's return home, we were all
to learn of George's untimely death in Belgium.
George had died as a result of his own very different
war while fighting in France on the Western Front.

Named after Edwin Senior's brother, their Uncle
George, the circumstances surrounding George's
death were vague and never really came to light. The
first Agnes knew about it was one day when I was
there visiting with Florence. We were in the kitchen

and Agnes was washing clothes in the sink as we chatted away, when suddenly her daughter Frances came running in to the kitchen from the hall shouting, 'Mum, Mum, there is a man at the door who looks like Daddy.'

Agnes wiped her hands on her apron and turned to me with anticipated joy. I followed her as she raced through to the hall, only to see a man in a Post Office uniform standing on the doorstep with his cap in his hand. With his other hand he held out a telegram. In a matter of seconds, and as realisation poured into her body, her emotions crashed from absolute elation to the most devastating loss. Her legs collapsed beneath her. Her freshly-wiped washday hands tried to break her fall but she hit the tiled floor, her body slamming against the ground with a deep, lingering, resounding thump. It was 10th April 1918 that he died, he was just thirty-four years old, and his life had been extinguished. Service number 40832, he had been fighting with the 3rd Battalion of the Worcestershire regiment since 1914, and when he died the war had been just seven months and one day away from its Armistice.

Seven months and one day – such a short time and yet also a lifetime: time enough to survive; time enough to die.

George, our dear, gentle George, had joined the ranks of the 'Glorious dead.'

The telegram was brief:

'It is my painful duty to inform you that a report has this day been received from the War Office notifying the death of George Cogbill, No. 40832, of the 3rd Worcestershire Regiment which occurred on April 10th 1918.

I am to express to you the sympathy and regret of the Army Council at your loss. The cause of death was – Killed in Action.'

The letter went on to inform Agnes that, should any personal effects be found, they would be forwarded to her at a later date. She never received anything from them, except for his service medals once the war was over.

Just as with Edwin, we had no body to help us to emotionally mourn George's loss. It felt as though we were constantly in a situation whereby we mourned a succession of empty spaces. George had left the comfort of his comfortable family life, and his homeland, to go and fight in someone else's bloody war, and there was no way Agnes would ever be able to bring him home to rest in his home country. He would never again walk in the steps of his forefathers or drink beer with his brothers. That last time he had left for the continent, he was destined to never return to his wife and children, and to never hold them in his arms and tell them he loved them.

Agnes was surprisingly strong – strong for the children, strong for Jack, strong for Mary-Ann and Edwin – all through the church service we organised in his memory, and the few weeks that followed. And then, thud, months later it dawned on her that that was all she would ever have, the time she had had with him when they were a young couple full of joy and hope for the future, and the time they had together when the girls were young.

Over time, though, Agnes regained that inner strength and, as the only breadwinner, she worked for Cadbury for a number of years, and then eventually she took over the running of her mother's local shop. She had come from a line of strong women and she knew she had to pick up the pieces and move on. In the end, I think she did that much better than any of us did.

We tried to help Mary-Ann, to console her and keep her busy, but her mourning lasted, well, it lasted until the day she died, which was twenty years later.

No one ever anticipated when they were having children back in the late 1800s that so many of them would be outlived by their parents. Mary-Ann's actions became automatic, her eyes distant, and I didn't see her truly happy ever again.

While Edwin had been her favourite son, of that there was no doubt, the one she had known the longest was George – her first-born. He was the one who had helped her when all the others had come along. He was the one she had depended on when Edwin Senior was out working, and she had had a multitude of other children to feed and keep clean. George had been there to help her mop up the pieces of the horrific losses of her tiny babies. Likewise, she had been there for George and Agnes when they had lost their own baby boy, and me when I lost little Adeline.

So many poor, poor, sick babies.

While many men did return – many more than those who died – the war spared few, for if it didn't take a person's life, then, for soldiers like Jack who had been physically fit when they left the battlefields behind, psychologically it remained with them for the rest of their life. This was what we had to contend with in each day that followed, and in George's loss Jack had now lost the one person he had looked up to. Henry was still in Canada, and we wrote to let him know about George. It must have been extremely difficult for him finding out about Edwin and George while he was so far away from the rest of us.

Jack descended into a place where no one could reach him. He had lost two of his brothers and he still had Alfred away fighting this wretched war which was dragging on and on. My own two brothers were still in India, and our wondering about the safety of them all lingered on and on.

I would take Florence with me to see Agnes and the girls. As the winter days turned into warmer spring days, and then those days turned into a long, hot summer, we would sit on the bench in the park watching the girls playing tag, and little Ted as he raced around, chasing them and nipping playfully at their heels like some demented herding collie, rather than the small terrier with the large attitude that he was. The children squealed in rapturous joy, while he bowed down in playful stances, and we laughed big belly laughs like there was no war; like the war was not still raging; like there were so many reasons to laugh. Mary-Ann, Edwin Senior, and even Jack, came along with us sometimes, and Edwin Senior joined Ted with chasing the girls, and he sometimes hid behind trees whose trunks were far too narrow to hide behind, and the girls squealed with pleasure at the antics of their grandfather as he let his guard down and allowed his own worries to dissolve into the warmth of summer.

When I look back now, I can see that this kind man,

Edwin Senior, was the backbone of the family and the one person who stopped the family from disintegrating. I don't think I realised that at the time, but this considerate man, he held us together, he was robust – hearty and made of the glue which bound us all. While Agnes' daughters had lost their father, Jack was no longer capable of being the father Florence had dreamed of having, however much we both wanted him to be. I'm sure, though, that underneath everything he had been through, and the impenetrable wall it had left behind, surely that was what Jack had wanted too?

Edwin had unintentionally become the father figure to all three of them. They had become *his girls*, he was the man who would be there for them as they ascended into adulthood, and who would give them the love they deserved. Agnes' own father had died before the war, so her two only had Edwin around, and, while my own father was there for Florence, he could be aloof, and his military training made him appear frightening. He and his new wife, Emma, had pictures around the house with him in his uniform – I think he liked to remember himself in his glory days when he was a powerful sergeant, and Florence had had her fill of the military in her short life... with Edwin she could relax and be herself.

On November 11th at 11am, the war finally came to a

close. Having lost so much, it seemed bittersweet, but as the news filtered through to us that it was true, the Allies had broken through enemy lines and treaties had been signed, we realised that this was it; after more than four very long years, the war really was over, and in hordes we lined the streets of Birmingham to celebrate.

How must those men who were still at The Front have felt, when gradually the skies became silent as the guns released their final loads, and arms were laid down? How long must it take, after having been under potential attack for so long, for you to believe there was peace at last and that your enemy could be trusted? That you could trust that the man who had been aiming a gun at you just the day before was no longer someone you had to kill? That the man in that trench, or lurking in an abandoned stone cottage, or hiding in the undergrowth beneath the broadleaved trees, was a person who, in years to come, you might pass in a Birmingham or Berlin street and not give a second glance?

For they really were just like us...

No more would the soldiers have to cower, duck and dive for fear of death. The men were coming home.

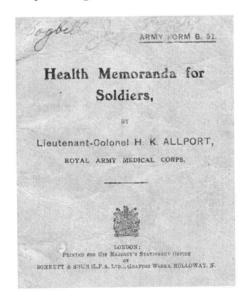

Jack Cogbill's attestation card

Jack's copy of the health care instructions

The Royal Garrison Artillery (RGA) Record Office
response to Grace's communications

Chapter 7

1918–1924

Jack struggled with his conscience; he was an ordinary, gentle, loving person who had brandished a gun. Like millions of others, he was someone who had been forced into killing; he was not a fighter, neither in stature nor mental constitution. Whether he was weak before he left, I don't think we'll ever know, but he went to fight in a foreign climate that was alien to his body, and I suppose he didn't cope as well as others did. In the end, for a chocolate worker from Bournville, the war was just too much to bear. I tried to help him, Good Lord, how I tried to get my Jack back, but that image I had seen of him on the day I'd walked into the hospital when he first returned from Salonica – that image of nothingness in his eyes – I think that, in the end anyway, that never went away.

Many men returned from the war suffering from what we called 'shell shock'. Jack was one of those men, and those remnants of the war remained with him until the day he died. I remember reading in a book on one of my far too frequent visits to the library, that by 1916 around forty percent of casualties in war zones were suffering from this strange condition.

Shell shock was thought to have been due to the traumatic sounds of bombs falling and other physical war stress but, whatever it was, something caused this mental breakdown of the soldiers. I used to see them all the time – you could spot them from a mile away – men walking around the streets automating their walking and talking. You could tell there were things that only they knew. They could only understand one another; those of us who hadn't been there could never really understand what they had gone through. Jack started to frequent the public house, as that was where he could meet up with other ex-service men, and they could whisper freely about what they had experienced. It eased the pressure for them. The pubs also provided them with the beer and liquor which would numb their memories: they found solace at the bottom of a bottle.

While the men met in the alehouses, we women would seek out companionship by meeting in the parks with the children, through chatting over the garden walls which separated our terraced houses or, when out fetching our groceries, we could stand in the street and swap our secrets. We spoke of the men who had returned with an altered state of mind, our husbands, brothers and sons who had come back from war quite different to how they had been when they left. We wanted them to share with us what had happened, so we could understand, but then, was there something in the way we consoled them and asked them to tell us more, some slight glance or subtle aspect of our body language, which told them that we didn't *really* want to know? Is that why they would never tell us what happened? Was it because, underneath it all, we wouldn't have been able to have coped with what they had to tell us? When all was said and done, perhaps we really didn't want to know in case it changed the way we felt about them. The husband or other loved one becoming someone who had taken another person's life is not something any of us would have taken lightly.

There *were* those who spoke more openly about what happened to them; by sharing their experiences it seemed they were able perhaps to let go a little; allowing themselves to discuss what they had seen or been involved with enabled them, in some way, to make sense of it all, but those men seemed to be few and far between. There were also those who wrote of what they had seen and experienced, and then stored their notes away from the world, until many years later when, after their death, those notes were found by their families. They were perhaps the canniest ones, as their memories were transferred to paper and then confined in some dark, wooden box for the rest of their days.

Then there were those soldiers like Jack, soldiers who never spoke of or wrote about the atrocities in which they had been involved, eventually taking their desperate tales with them to the grave. They never told anyone what happened, but the evidence of the horrors they had experienced were etched on their faces and demonstrated through their actions, in everything they said and everything they did. The gentle person Jack had been before he left seemed to have dissolved into a dreadful impression of war. He had undergone a shift in his personality, becoming irritable and short-tempered.

Jack was also very bored – and this boredom didn't help his state of mind. With his epilepsy it was difficult for him to work. To help us out with money, I went to work in the screw works factory a few streets away, and Mary Ann looked after Florence. They adored each other. Florence used to help her with her baking, and preserving of foods Edwin Senior had grown in the garden. Once they had finished their kitchen chores, they would take Ted to the River Rea and throw a stick for him to fetch.

Some days when I went to collect Florence and Ted, I would find them all next to the river and the two of them would be laughing and having fun while Ted raced in and out of the river retrieving sticks which were far too big for the grip of his tiny terrier jaws. I was tired from the work I had been doing at the factory, but as we walked home Florence brightencd my day with her tales of all she had been doing at Granny and Grandpa's; meanwhile Ted marched along beside us, strutting his small chest at any other dogs who dared to look his way.

When Florence started school, it was Mary-Ann and Edwin, along with little Ted, who used to meet her at the school gates and then take her back to their house until I collected her. That time away from home became almost idyllic; it was the time when we could be ourselves. Jack would sometimes amble down to the school gates to be there when Florence came out of school, but those times were rare.

A cloud had descended at home, and in the middle of the night Jack invariably woke up screaming; his body shaking uncontrollably. He wasn't cold; he wasn't always particularly hot when it happened, he was simply reliving whatever he had seen, heard... and done.

Being a gunner meant he would have had to have fired a gun – I knew that much, but who shot first? Was it a matter of whoever saw the enemy on either side first had a go at killing the other, or did they wait a moment for the time it takes for a heart to beat to see who would dare first? How does a soldier, whatever side they are on, equate that memory of killing in their future life when they have returned to their family? Was it in silence that most of them reckoned everything out when they got back? Was this what Jack would be like until the day he died? When he woke like that and I switched on a light I would find him curled in the foetal position enshrouded in sweat, or sat bolt upright with his eyes glazed in terror. He had returned from the war wearing the evidence of his hurt and pain like some grotesque mask. They were difficult times for all of us, and I would try to reach him to get him to stop, lest his cries woke little Florence who was sleeping in the room next to ours.

When Jack's breakdowns happened during the day, Florence used to run and hide in the garden; the gentle man she had known before had disappeared from her world when he had left British shores in 1917. But little Ted, sometimes it seemed he could reach out to Jack better than any of us. I would often find Jack sitting in his old, green armchair staring into the distance; silent and completely still, except for one hand which was gently caressing Ted's head and ears. Whatever had happened in Salonica, he was never going to fully share it with me, but Ted, sometimes I felt that if Ted could have asked him, he would have told Ted.

Alfred, and my brothers, Bill and Tom, were finally demobilised from the war in early 1919. They returned to us as war heroes and, as such, they were immediately eligible for assistance with re-establishing themselves on "Civvy Street". For Jack, however, there was doubt about his eligibility for a war pension due to his early return from Salonica, and he began a new battle, this time to justify his case to the Ministry for War and Pensions.

Both my brothers had acquired a taste for the military. Just like Father, there was something about life in the forces – the unpredictability of it, perhaps, which drew them back into joining up and both of them remained in the forces for many years.

The vast majority of men who survived the war, and were eventually demobilized, returned to the jobs they had done before the conflict began and, as employers who were renowned for their great tendency to be concerned about the welfare of their workers, Cadbury was exceptional. Where men had returned and were deemed no longer suitable for the type of work they had done before – whether through shellshock or other more obvious physical injuries, they were offered assistance in finding more suitable work. When the effects had been so great that those men were unable to work at all, they were offered counselling and convalescent home support to help them to recover. Jack's trait was such that he did not like to discuss what had happened – whether he ever managed to open up to the people who were helping him I'll never know, but what I do know is that the counselling didn't really seem to help him. Sometimes, for a day or two after he had been given some support, his mood seemed a little lighter, but that mood often did not last.

Many of us women had changed too – we had been without our men for several years and their return was difficult for us. We had got into routines which did not involve their being in our lives; our children, too, they had forgotten what it was like to have a man in the house. Suddenly there was an air of masculinity again, and in some cases the man's return brought an unwelcome domineering presence; the gentle matriarchal way that things had been while the husband had been away often became a much more turbulent environment. I suppose in many ways that was how it was with Jack; he was not deliberately hostile, but the problems he had brought back with him created something which was at times, I'm afraid to say, well, I think you could only describe it as being intimidating. He wasn't intentionally argumentative; it was just that the things which had never bothered him before seemed to irritate him with an intensity that worried me.

Florence could not always hear what he said, and it wasn't until many years later we discovered she had problems with her hearing – somehow she had covered up her deafness with coping strategies, however, if she didn't respond when Jack asked her to do something, he would bang the table, hit the wall, or throw something across the room. He never hurt her physically though – even the Jack who returned from the war was never deliberately cruel. He did retain an element of the compassionate man he had been, it was just that sometimes that part of him was difficult to see.

Things had changed for women in general; we had been empowered by the Suffragettes' movement. They had fought long and hard for us from the late 1890s and into the new century, but for so very long – three long decades, reform of the laws on voting for women didn't come. It was unacceptable that we should be treated as though we were second-class citizens to our men. It was only when the government saw what women were capable of; how we had kept the country going, industry and all, in the absence of so many men, that in 1918 we were granted the vote, but unfortunately there was still inequality. Even then, after all that we had suffered together, men could vote at eighteen, but women had to be thirty. It was much later, a decade in fact, before we were considered to be equal to men. To be honest, many women I knew were so subservient through years of being under the control of their fathers or husbands, that the introduction of the vote for women didn't make such a difference unless you were middle or upper class, but it was all about the option to vote if we wanted to. That's what it meant for me, anyway, and whether my friends voted or not, it was something I always did.

Some aspects of life started to amass a level of normality. Young Frank went to work for Cadbury. Because of his illness Jack was never able to return there, but with Frank working there he got to hear some news from the people he used to work with. Following the war, in 1919 Cadbury merged with JS Fry and Sons, and the company gained an even greater presence, not just locally, but worldwide. As it expanded, so, too, did other industries and Birmingham became a hive of industry.

Meanwhile, there remained some stigma attached to the war in Salonica, and this affected Jack in a detrimental way. Even Alfred still doubted that Jack's war in Salonica had been such that it should have caused the signs he was showing. There were times when I resented Alfred's visits because he seemed to feel that in some petty way his war had been more important than Jack's. His implications made me angry, especially when he used to tell Jack he should 'pull himself together.' I felt I didn't know enough about it to defend Jack and, of course, Jack wasn't telling anyone anything about what had happened over there, and so, over the years I have tried to build a picture of what happened in Salonica and tried to understand why Jack became the way he was when he returned.

Initially it was hard to find out anything particularly tangible. As I explored the pages of diaries and books officers had written about the Great War, I found that Salonica was barely mentioned in anything I read. I went to the library whenever I got the chance and searched text after text about the war – I may have found a page or two here and there about Salonica, but there was no great sense in what I found to read that anything really important to the war happened there.

Some of the writers marvelled at the scenery of Macedonia and the social aspects of life in Salonica, including the bars and clubs. There was talk of plays and dances; aspects of a war foreign to the image of war we hear about and see in books, and I got the impression that, at first anyway, when the troops had arrived, not much had happened over there and there had been plenty of time to go and see 'the sights'. It was as though it were some free holiday provided for the men courtesy of the government. Perhaps the books were referring to the officers, and not the ordinary soldiers, however, the more I read, the more despondent I became. Was it really true that so little of the war had happened in Salonica that no one ever thought it necessary to speak out about its atrocities?

It puzzled me, therefore, why Jack had suffered so much, and why he came back from the war and experienced the years of night terrors and intolerable flashbacks, when it seemed as though what was going on over there was something akin to some strange camp from which wives and families were excluded. Indeed, many reports I found suggested that, in spite of initial good intentions by the British government, the action in Salonica proved in the end to be of little use to the overall war effort – it seemed to become very much a stalemate.

As time went by, it became an obsession for me to find some tiny piece of information which would confirm why Jack had become how he was, just a tiny piece of information which would corroborate what I saw at home every day. And then, finally, and after months of searching, I discovered what could have contributed to Jack's post-war problems...

In the main library in the centre of town, after having leafed through reams and reams of books and journals, I came across a 1918 report about WW1 activity in Macedonia and surrounding areas. It had been written by a war correspondent – someone who had actually been in Salonica and breathed the same air as Jack. He wrote that during the war people's opinions were such that Salonica was a "picnic" for the men. What he had written afterwards made my heart beat more quickly and I swiftly went to ask the librarian for a pen and paper so I could copy down what the book said. He went on to declare in the battalions' defence that, "the idea that the soldier lives an easy and safe life in Macedonia is absurdly false. There is very little leave for the soldier in the Balkans. There are battalions which have been in the front line for seven months without relief, and when you consider that our trenches are shelled every day and that patrols go out every night, seven months needs a good deal of luck to get through without being hurt."

I carefully wrote out his article, word for word, and kept it so that whenever Jack was having a particularly bad time, I could take it out of the wooden box, carefully unfold it and then read it quietly to myself, all the time trying to understand a little of what he had experienced. It transpired that, in the author's opinion anyway, the conditions there were just as difficult as they had been on the Western Front, and that they were further complicated by the hilly, rough ground which the men had to traipse through on a daily basis, much of the time having to avoid shells and gunfire as they went about their duties.

For his time in Greece Jack was based on the Doiran Front, where the Allies' trenches traversed the border between Serbia and Greece. The Allied armies based there lived as one unit, and side by side they fought together: the British, French, Russian, Serbian, Algerian, Italian, Turkish, Albanian, Greek, Indian, and Balkan soldiers – they were all there, facing the enemy's forces together.

Jack was one of the many soldiers who had arrived in Greece as reinforcements to the Allies who had been based there since October 1915. In December 1916, when his Battalion arrived, the war on the Balkan Front was inactive – a forced inactivity due to the weather which had resulted in excess mud on the barren, hilly terrain. The lull during this time was when the Allies planned their spring offensive against the Bulgarians. The Doiran Front, along the banks of Lake Doiran, was to be a part of the Allies' plan.

In 1917, a massive fire spread through Salonica, destroying almost a square mile of its buildings and leaving many thousands of people homeless. When Jack was in a talkative mood and I asked him about the town of Salonica itself, he said he knew very little about it because his time there was spent at The Front. In his letters he had never spoken of bars and clubs and so on, just of the men and the trenches and how they were all getting along with one another – anything he was allowed to tell me without his letter being confiscated anyway – banal information which now seems insignificant; pages of things I didn't need to know, but which at the time had given me the hope I needed to carry on to be strong for Florence.

Jack told me that when he arrived there in 1916 he was astounded by the beauty of the large houses along the sea front and, as their ship had approached the quay, he had wondered how such a beautiful city could be at war. Finally, after many days of rough ocean waves, they were on terra firma once more. They marched through the city and headed straight to The Front. He and the rest of the soldiers of his rank hardly saw the city after that.

In that August of 1917, when they had seen the orange glow in the sky as the flames raged through the city for almost two weeks, they had felt saddened by the catastrophe of it all. They had assumed it was something to do with the war that had caused the fire, but when it turned out that it had started with a simple kitchen fire, in many ways it made it seem even more of a tragedy that, with all the deliberate destruction going on, a small fire could escalate and cause such widespread devastation. Some of the troops were ordered to the city to help to rescue people, and attempt to extinguish the fire, but as a gunner, Jack was one of those who had to remain defending the lines.

It is hard to imagine, but over four hundred thousand members of the British forces served in Salonica at some point during the war. Of these, the Allies suffered around ten and a half thousand losses. Many of these deaths were because of diseases such as malaria, which was particularly rife because of the mosquitoes which thrived in the Greek climate. With great ease a mosquito would transmit the tiny parasites when it injected its proboscis into some unfortunate victim. Watching people dying around you in the heat of the Mediterranean sun, that can't have been easy for anyone, but I suppose for someone like Jack, seeing all that, and in addition, knowing you had this strange condition which caused you to have convulsions with no warning; that must have been especially hard for him.

Through reading about Salonica and knowing more about what Jack had experienced, it became easier for me to cope with everyday life. It was as though I was nursing someone with a long term illness, only the illness he suffered from you couldn't see. Soldiers who returned with limps were offered sympathy, a seat, and a cup of tea as they hobbled along the streets; soldiers like Jack were treated with disdain and sometimes fear. You didn't know how he would react, you see, sometimes he could find a laugh which would spontaneously rise from somewhere deep inside him, but most often his actions and reactions were noted through their absence.

My sister Leah was like a welcome breeze on a scorching hot day. She was a person who, when she entered a room, she brightened it with her vibrant nature, but the death of our mother back before the war had hit her hard and she stopped eating as well as she should have been doing. She had helped me a lot with Jack and, just like everyone else did, he seemed to have a soft spot for her. Sometimes she would come over and sit at the table reading poetry to us all. She loved poetry and wrote some of her own. Jack would sit there listening to her, absorbing the essence of her ways and how the light seemed to dance around her as her voice calmly soothed us all; wiping away the past and easing us into our future.

Children and animals loved Leah and seemed to crave her company. Florence used to sit beside her beholding her as though she were some kind of angel, while Ted was equally enthralled by her presence and, if ever a dog could have spoken, then Ted would have let her know – instead he did it with his eyes and the way he relaxed next to her, seemingly listening to her every word.

After knowing Leah and loving her for the whole of her short life, suddenly she was gone from our lives, and we wondered at the cruel, cruel fate or supernatural force that had taken her away from us.

Had we not suffered enough? We had thanked our

lucky stars that our family had not been affected by influenza but, letting down our guard, we had forgotten about the disease which had blighted so many families in the time leading up to the war. Tuberculosis – it had not gone away, it had always been there, lurking in the background to come and steal another one of us. Whether she would have fared better had she still had our mother around, I suppose we'll never know, but she certainly struggled without her and that must have made her more susceptible to the callous wrath of such an infection – how could these paltry, tiny organisms leave such catastrophe in their wake?

She died on 24th July 1922, and was just seventeen years old, so very, very young. She had been ill for some time with a hacking cough which gave her the most severe chest and back pain. She had nasty, yellow-green, mucoid phlegm, which she sporadically coughed up, often with blood. We knew it was tuberculosis and had seen others die from it, but we hoped that because she was young and strong she would beat it. My brother, Bill, made her concoctions of herbs and other remedies, but she was too far gone.

It was my birthday three days before she died, and we sat around her bed praying and hoping, but the war and all its poverty and destruction had reaped the most beautiful of people and even then, four years after its end, it was still taking. As Bill eagerly reached forward with a cup of steaming greenness, she pathetically tried to lift her head and shoulders on her now almost-emaciated body and, on smelling the green brew in the cup, she turned her head to the side and coughed up the reddest of blood, her body convulsing with each breath she tried to take.

Realising she had the strength to neither lift her body nor swallow what he was offering, she lay her head back on the pillow and reached to wipe the red froth from her face; and then the faintest, most haunting smile crossed her pallid face as she looked deep into Bill's eyes. Tuberculosis had come to claim her life, and there was nothing any one of us could do to stop it. Suddenly, it seemed that she was calmly accepting of her fate, while we, well, we were unwilling to let her go.

Flourishing in the unsanitary conditions of the war, in the time leading up to the war it had particularly placed poor people at risk of infection. We weren't well off, but because of Father we had fared better than many during the war, so why had this happened to her? This bacterium was passed between people through the air, just by coughing or sneezing. It was indiscriminate – it chose who it wanted and made its way into their body without remorse. And it had chosen Leah.

We used to call tuberculosis 'the consumption'

because of how it used to seem to devour, or 'consume' people, and it was particularly rife back then until antibiotics, along with the increased use of the vaccine, halted its spread, but when Leah was sick there was nothing we could do except wait and hope.

Before she became sick she had been having bad toothache and had gone to the dentist to get the offending tooth removed. I've often wondered whether that was the start of it, you know, whether it was having the dental treatment that infected her. I suppose we shall never know.

For three long days she had clung to life, sometimes accepting the smallest sip of water, and then, as the sunshine seeped through the windows, casting its light across her pale, elfin-like face, she faded away; as she had been helpful during life, she made it easy for those of us waiting at her bedside by drifting away while she slept.

'She's gone,' Bill whispered as he came into the room with yet another remedy to make her passing easy. He had given up on trying to save her after the steaming green concoction affair, but he had brought along a variety of herbal remedies to help her to sleep and to ease her coughs. And they had helped, they really had, but here, she was gone.

Simultaneously dealing with my grief at the loss of my sister and trying to help Jack deal with the phantoms in his mind and the loss of his two brothers, I got on with my life, taking great care of my dear, sweet daughter, Florence; constantly shielding her from the terrors Jack was experiencing.

In 1924, my brother Bill and his wife, Hilda, had a son. At last a new post-war generation was beginning and there was hope that they would make a better job of things than we, their parents, had. I immediately liked Hilda the moment I met her – she had a warm heart and was someone I could easily relate to. Her house was always welcoming, full of laughter and plenty of food she had made to share with her guests. In the years that followed, I spent a lot of time there, and in some ways she helped to fill the gaping hole left by my losing Leah.

My sister Florrie had become more and more distant from me as time had passed. I sensed she felt awkward round Jack, and he was my priority. I hadn't seen her for many months, perhaps as long as a year, and even in the few years before that our meetings had been sporadic. She was working as a nurse and I missed her. I don't know what went wrong between us, but when Tom returned from India, he told me that, just months before, he had received a letter from her in which she said she felt I didn't care about her. How could she have thought such a thing? I think Tom was trying hard to repair our ever-fracturing family, but it seems his efforts were to no avail.

Florrie and me, we did meet up again a few times and things were quite frosty, but when eventually she went to live in America, it was hard to keep up the contact.

Tom and Bill had always blamed Father for Mother's premature death – I don't know why, but they felt that he should have been nicer to her. Father was always impatient with her and her death was a turning point in Tom and Bill's relationship with Father as they found it very difficult to be around him again after that. Our fractured family became even more fragmented than it had ever been. Many years after the First World War, Tom came back from serving in the Commonwealth and was employed by the steelworks, working in the same factory as me – he carried on doing that for many years.

Our ongoing battle with the Pensions Office came to an end when it was agreed that Jack's full-blown epilepsy was due to the war and its effects on him. It was January 1924 and he was finally notified that he would be awarded a pension. They confirmed that his condition had been caused by service. It was something he had clung to for so long. He had constantly wanted to prove to everyone that his illness had been exacerbated by the war, and here it was, at last he could tell the world – we both could.

For so long people had cast doubt over Jack's integrity and why he had come home in advance of the end of the conflict, and at last we had some evidence, right there in front of us on a piece of paper. It lifted his spirits for a short time – I suppose it was bound to, but it wasn't long before he was back to how he had been before.

The fact that this confirmation came six years after Jack returned from Salonica infuriated me – we had six years of not knowing or understanding what was going on and whether he had been affected by his time in Greece, or whether he was imagining his symptoms! We knew there was something terribly wrong with him, but for us to have to wait six years for this to be confirmed was very difficult for us.

I suppose it was possible that at the time of his joining the service there HAD been some underlying problem which had made him more prone to the effects of the heat. Perhaps there was something, some imbalance or weakness that made him simply more vulnerable and less able to cope in those extreme temperatures? We knew he was having some symptoms before he left, but there was never any doubt in my mind that whatever he experienced over there had made him worse, and that it greatly contributed to his demise.

Chapter 8

1925 – Jack

It must have been 1924 or 1925 when, one cold winter's night, Jack returned home following an evening at the public house on the corner of the next street. I was ready for bed and just about to go upstairs. As he pushed open the front door I saw his warm breath on the gust of cold air before I caught sight of his face, but as soon as I saw him I could see straight away that something terrible had happened to him. He was shaking uncontrollably and was on the verge of tears. This was more than too much ale – he was clearly desperately upset about something! I took hold of his arm and led him to a chair beside the kitchen table.

'Jack, Jack, whatever is wrong.' I repeated over and over to him.

He in front of me with that same look I remembered seeing on Edwin's friend Robert's face that day in the church, just weeks before he had ended his own life. As my heart jolted, he bowed his head and began to sob. With each movement of his chest he let out an inhuman noise like that of a prey animal meeting its fate in the jaws of a large predator; an animal in the last throes of its life.

This continued for over an hour, and I was on the

point of rushing next door to ask my neighbor, Irene, to go and fetch a doctor when, finally, he began to speak.

The look of fear still etched in his face (was that now-familiar look the reflection of a memory of the horror of the battlefield? I couldn't decide), I sat down beside him and reached out to hold onto his hand. 'Grace, it was awful, so, so terrible.'

He inhaled slowly and deeply, taking in as much air as his lungs could hold, and then went on with his story, 'I saw Edmund. You'll remember him – he used to be friends with George. After the war he came back to Blighty, but because his mother had died of influenza, he went to live up north to be near an aunt of his. That's why we had never seen him again. I always assumed he must have been killed, you know, missing in action and no one had ever seemed to know for sure what had happened to him...' He paused for a breath, looked down into his lap, then back up at me, and continued.

'They killed them Grace.' And then he stopped again as tears filled his eyes and he inhaled deeply and then slowly let the air out again. I could smell beer on his breath.

'Who, Jack? Who did they kill?'

'Walter, Jack, Egbert, and two others,' he blurted out

– the stench of alcohol still lingering like a wall between us.

At first I thought he wasn't making any sense, but then I remembered, those men had been in George's regiment; they had gone off to The Front right at the beginning of the war – they left at the same time as George. Egbert was one of his good friends – he, too, had been married with a young family. 'I know, Jack,' I reassured him, 'I know… they were killed in the war.' *This was obviously one of his confused periods,* I thought, but then he pulled his hand away from underneath mine; his brow furrowed and his face took on a look that had become all too familiar, and then he impatiently continued with his story.

'No, Grace, you don't understand. They weren't killed by the enemy. They were killed by us, we British, one dawn in July, 1915. We killed them Grace, no one else.' He was absolutely insistent and willing me to understand what he was telling me. His voice sounded choked, but through his broken words I eventually gleaned that Edmund had told him that, at dawn one day in July 1915, five of the soldiers from George's regiment had been punished by being shot by a firing squad. All five had tried to desert the army and been captured. Edmund had known all of them, and as he had consumed more and more alcohol earlier that evening, while at first he and Jack had reminisced about the times before the war, it was inevitable that in the end they would talk about their respective war experiences.

Edmund had become more and more talkative, and the secrets he had harboured became easier for him to share as the drink flowed and numbed his senses, giving him the freedom to let go of his story. He said he had never told anyone since the war; that he had kept it securely locked inside his mind. At the end of the evening Edmund had thanked Jack and told him that he felt better now; better that he had been able to share the details of this atrocity.

Some things are better left unsaid, and while I could understand the devastation of this poor man with his memories, I could not forgive him for telling Jack – Jack had his own terrors to bear. There was a change for the worse in Jack after his chance meeting with Edmund, and he took on the look of someone who had given up, as though he felt life was no longer worth living. I truly believe he lost his faith in human nature that night. Edmund headed back to his northern town and we never saw him again, but the knowledge of what had happened, well, you can't take that back, can you? Once something has been said it remains in your subconscious eating away at you. You may think it has gone and that it will never make its way back to the forefront of your mind, and then one day it reappears and gnaws away at your soul, stealing it little by little until there's nothing left.

Once we eventually managed to get to bed, when all the talking was done but the sick feeling deep in my gut lingered, I lay on my back with my eyes wide open, staring at the intermittent, alternating flecks of brightness and leaf-shaped shadows which leisurely danced across the ceiling. The yellow glow of light was being projected over the top of the curtains from the street lamps outside.

Each time I closed my eyes the leafy shadows were replaced by that of the five men tied to posts; their terrified gazes fixed on the ends of the rifles which were aiming straight for their hearts. Their decision to not be blindfolded was their final tribute of bravery to a war they no longer wanted to be a part of. But this? This was not the alternative they had imagined possible when their escape had been so meticulously planned. White cloths, intended to ensure the unwilling perpetrators did not miss their targets, had already been pinned to the chests of the men by a medical officer – a clear 'X' marking the spot which would kill immediately – so long as the aim of the rifle was straight.

The soldiers, pausing with their rifles poised, took no comfort from the fact that they had been informed that a blank cartridge had been inserted inside the chamber of one of their rifles, so no man would know for sure whether he had shot one of his own: his colleague; his friend; his brother. In the backs of their minds, however, they stored the thought that surely if they fired a blank cartridge it would feel different to them than live ammunition would?

Their hands shook in synchronicity with the trembling of their legs as they waited for the command which would alter the course of the rest of their lives – each man knowing this would be one day they would never forget. When eventually I drifted to sleep, I witnessed images of men slumping to the ground as their bodies became lifeless. Egbert's face came into view and his vacant eyes met mine, his brow was relaxed as his nerve endings had lost the will to protest. The image of his cold stare reverberated through me and I woke with a jolt, while the lights on the ceiling still danced their slow, sporadic waltz.

Jack stirred in his sleep – his slumber, like mine, affected by images of war, but for him it induced memories, while mine were simple imaginings of how things may have happened. He tossed and turned, his face contorted as it often was while he slept, but it looked even more so in the dancing yellow light.

Knowing that sleep was not going to swathe me in its warm cloak that night, I gently woke Jack and rescued him from his disturbed sleep. We eased our way out of bed and held hands as we left the bedroom – taking ourselves far, far away from the tomb of nightmares. Down the stairs we went, and on into the sitting room where we lit a lamp and wrapped ourselves in blankets and drank hot tea; silent and, for once, companionable, in the temporary womb we had created for ourselves. I noticed there were deep, dark shadows now permanently nestled under Jack's eyes, and he was paler than I had ever seen him.

He stopped going out after that night, and his demeanour was shattered. Somewhere in him the light that had occasionally begun to shine again; the feeling that I was getting my old Jack back, that was gone.

Before Jack left for war he had to write a will – they all did, all the men who were going off to fight. Most wills, like Jack's, were simple, and stated that in the event of their death they would leave the whole of their estate to their wife or parents. Jack's was made out on the 11th December 1916, the day before he went away to Salonica, and it was signed by the District Registrar. This was a routine, almost clinical, way of dealing with the matter of potential death. It was easier to get the men to sign before they left and know that, if they should die, their estate would be distributed as they had wished and that there would be minimal paperwork to do back home. Before he left, he had told me his will had been written and everything was left to me in the event of him not returning from the war. I never wanted to believe that the war would take him; I imagine that none of us expected that our men would not come back. There was a sense that we were protected somehow – that we were immune to catastrophe, and even when Edwin and George were killed, I still felt that the war would not take my Jack – and it didn't, not then anyway.

His epilepsy was getting worse. He had developed some extremely worrying symptoms in that he sometimes had to reach out to stop himself from falling when he was navigating his way around the house. He thought I had been moving the furniture around and that was why he was struggling. I hadn't, though, and I knew that something more than his troubles in Salonica were now taking place. His speech was sometimes incoherent, and it made him more irritable than normal when he tried to explain something to me. He fought back against the demons in his head, but in the end it was all too much for him. Weeks passed and I nagged him and nagged him to go and see a doctor. Eventually he did, and within hours he was sent to the hospital for an X-ray.

The diagnosis was perhaps something I had expected for a long time. If I had actually sat and added up all that had happened, then perhaps this was the conclusion I would have come to. There was a mass inside Jack's head.

Everything we had gone through together; all that he had experienced and the gradual worsening of his symptoms suddenly made sense... there was no doubt in any of the doctors' minds – the mass was a tumour in his brain. They let us have him home for a while, on the understanding that he neither climbed the stairs nor got over-excited, but that while was not long enough for, within weeks, he was back in hospital.

That time at home with him, well, he seemed different somehow. It seemed as though all the time he had spent brooding about the war and Salonica – all those demons in his head – they were all gone. He was still not my Jack, though, his movements were slow and automated and his speech was sparse and confused, but there was a look I could see in his eyes.

For a long time afterwards I puzzled over that look – but many years after he had passed away, when his face had haunted my dreams for so long, eventually I realised that that look was acceptance: acceptance of his fate; acceptance of all that he had done; acceptance of all that he had had to do. Amid that expression there was something else, though; his face had become almost child-like, as though he had regressed to some part of his youth that he had subconsciously kept only for himself – for the time when he would need that memory; the time when he would know he was about to die.

One day he passed out at home. He had been standing next to the sink, right there in front of me, and one second he was trying to tell me what he would like for dinner, and the next he was lying unconscious on the kitchen floor. I couldn't rouse him and, after I screamed out for help, Florence came running. She immediately saw what had happened, absorbing the whole scene in just a fraction of a second. The rest is a blur, only I remember an ambulance arriving, and within half an hour Jack was in a bed at Birmingham General Hospital. And this time I knew he would not be coming home.

The following day – a scorching hot, August day, I visited him. He was still unconscious, and for the rest of the day I sat holding his hand and willing him to talk to me, but there was nothing, and at 11pm on 20th August 1926, he passed away. He was just thirty-eight years old.

The following morning I woke to the sounds of blackbirds in the apple tree outside my window. With dear old Ted padding along beside me, I ventured outside onto the dew-covered grass to put some crumbs out beneath the tree for the birds. It was going to be another very hot day. Ted was already panting with the threat of the heat. He was very old now and had become less resilient to changes in temperature. He seemed to sense something was up – I guessed he was wondering about Jack and was picking up on the sadness which had descended on the house, and so I crouched down in front of him and held his head in my hands. His eyes could no longer see, but I stroked the side of his face and told him it was okay, 'you still have Florence and me, Ted, we'll be all right.' And with that, I fell down beside him, pulled him onto my lap, and sobbed into his wiry fur.

Eventually, when the blackbirds' cheerful conversations became louder and more anxious about the crumbs I'd scattered for them – they were clearly waiting for us to go back into the house – I eased myself from the ground and made my way back to the house where Florence was making breakfast for us both. Ted ambled behind following my scent and the echoes of my footsteps.

Later on that day I went to the Register Office to register Jack's death and, standing in the queue waiting to be told to take a seat, I felt a desolation piling on top of me – the war and all its destruction had destroyed what little time I had with Jack. When my name was called and I went through to the office with its stark, whitewashed walls, the registrar who filled in the form was sympathetic and allowed me to cry – I supposed they got used to that kind of thing.

The coroner's report said Jack had suffered from a very specific type of tumour – glioma cerebri. All the signs, such as the seizures and the mood changes he had been experiencing in the time before he died, had been a part of this. In some ways it helped me to understand more of what he had been going through, and I felt regretful for the times that I had been impatient with him and, I suppose, when I had expected more from him.

I'm sure, through peer pressure and society-induced bravado, that when Jack signed up there was intention on his behalf to cover up a condition which had already become symptomatic prior to leaving for foreign shores. I imagine the most likely explanation of his troubles in Salonica is that the full blown seizures were brought on by the extreme temperatures and conditions in which the men were having to work, and the tumour was something he developed in the years after the war had ended. There are so many questions which remain unanswered because Jack held his feelings in – hardly ever voicing what he felt or what he remembered. Was it Jack's brain tumour that changed him? Was it this that made him depressed, confused, angry, frightened? Perhaps… but also the war…

There is something ethereally omnipresent about losing the ones you love in summer. Standing beside a deep hole which has been dug in the ground for them, and watching their coffin being lowered into the earth, whilst in the trees you can hear the birds singing and the rustling of the summer leaves as the warm breeze kisses their edges, and you can feel the sun's heat on your face drying your tears, there is something which does not quite fit. Death by its very nature should be represented by rain, clouds and thunderous thunder crashing against the skies, but instead, the grey, stark skies of death days become some of the sunniest days of your life. On the outside, anyway. Inside, they are the days when you wish you were dead, too, and no measure of sunshine will make you think otherwise.

I had had my fill of summer deaths – my sweet baby Adeline had died in June of 1915, my sister Leah in July 1922, and now, my dear husband Jack in August 1926. With each of their deaths I had this feeling that it was not right to die when the world looked so beautiful – when there were flowers growing all around us, with butterflies and bees fluttering around them reaping pollen from within their depths; when the scents of freshly mown grass and honeysuckle lingered on the breeze; when the smells of freshly baked bread and biscuits wafted through the air as people opened their windows to allow their baking to cool; and there was laundry hanging on the line instead of next to the fire – this was the time of year when your clothes smelled of blossom and soap instead of the smoke from their drying next to your fire. How could anyone die on a day like that?

Although Jack died because of a brain tumour, and this explained a lot of what had happened over the preceding years, I always knew in my heart that he had experienced something in Salonica which had tortured his soul. I never wanted to believe that the doubters about the horror of the war in Salonica could be right; I never wanted to believe that 'his' war had been the Salonica which was so often the butt of post-war ridicule. I had lived through eight years with Jack when he returned from the war, and the actions of this haunted man mirrored the war that actually happened in his war in Salonica, rather than the one many would have chosen to believe. It was his war – Jack's war – his experiences and his own battles. When he returned those battles became much more personal, and he seemed to blame himself for everything that had happened: Adeline's death, George's death, Edwin's death, he even blamed himself for the war. Yes, there were times when I think that he, Jack Cogbill, believed he was personally responsible for the whole, blinking war.

All the inner turmoil and the guilt – it seems that the only escape from them was when he died. His face had lost the distorted look of a man in conflict with his own self – he was finally at peace. By this time Florence was almost thirteen, so she had known her father, but what she had known of him was tainted by the life he had experienced. How I hate that wretched war for taking away my Jack... not just my Jack, but Florence's Jack, too.

The consequences of a tumultuous time are far-reaching, and their effects are frequently felt for many decades in the future, not just for the individual, but for those around them – Jack's death and the shadow of the war, and the Second World War that followed, had a profound effect on all of us and the future we made for ourselves. Some would have given up; others flourished, relieved they could move on once the burden of a life they didn't sign up to was over; I suppose I did neither of these things and, instead, gave everything I had left to Florence and to you three, my dear grandchildren.

For Florence it was harder – her whole childhood had been consumed by the war. She had never known anything but strife for so many years. She didn't have the advantage I had of knowing that the world could be at peace; that it could be a wonderful, wonderful place. She had grown so quickly, and at Jack's funeral in dawned on me just how much she had grown. When I had not been concentrating, when my attention had been on working and looking after Jack, she had changed from my little girl into a beautiful young woman.

There were a lot of Irish people moving into the district. Your mother used to have plenty of potential suitors – she was beautiful, with dark, wavy hair and hazel eyes. She was slim and well-dressed; she could have won over virtually any young man she wanted.

The man who came to ask for my daughter's hand in marriage was a Birmingham-born young man of Irish parentage. As soon as I saw Robert Fegan walk along the street with a bouquet of flowers in his hand, I knew he was after her. He may have won over my daughter with that silver tongue of his, but he wasn't going to win me over. I would be steadfast in my decision – he was *not* going to marry my daughter.

Robert stood in front of me with his brown, wavy hair, handsome face, and a twinkle in his blue eyes. He flashed me a smile and, in spite of myself, I was bowled over by his presence – his aura – whatever it was he had. That was all he had to do, just stand there with his sparkling eyes, and I knew immediately that he was the one who would make my daughter happy.

He played us all tunes on his piano and his accordion – he was very talented at both, and I could see why Florence had fallen for him. I noticed straight away that he had an affinity with animals, and by then little Ted had passed away and I'd been without a dog for some years. But then, one day Robert turned up with a little tan terrier bitch he'd found scavenging around the stables when he had been working with the cart horses. I named her Penny, and she gave me many years of great company until a few years ago when she, too, passed away.

Robert had immediately brought a great deal of love back into all our lives, not just love, but the fun we had missed through Florence's childhood and youth. And so, eventually, the two of them got married.

It was a lovely day in December 1936 when they wed. Why so many of our family chose to marry in the cold, dark of winter, I don't know – perhaps, though, it was the cool cleanliness of the frost and snow, and how they seemed to wipe away the stuffiness of the summer's heat.

There is something incredibly romantic about going out into the cold on a freezing winter's day, when you are wrapped up warm and the cold kisses your pink cheeks. That was the type of day we had when they made their promise to one another to be together for the rest of their lives. Their wedding was attended by so many neighbours, friends and relatives and, for me anyway, I was able to sink into the moment and imagine, with great caution after all that had happened, the years to come and the possibilities that lay ahead.

Grace and Jack's daughter Florence Cogbill (to
become Fegan) and Robert Fegan (with the
accordion), with his younger brother, Jim, and collie
dog – 1930s

Florence Fegan (1955)

Chapter 9

Grace – War and hope

I need not have ever worried about Robert's suitability for Florence, for their marriage was immediately a happy one and, in time, the three of you came along, but when you were born, Maureen, this coincided with a time when the world was just about to enter its next great conflict. Just twenty-one years had passed since we had all felt, been determined, that we could not possibly allow such atrocities to happen again, and there we were, embroiled in something we could not control. To have to go through all that again seemed incomprehensible. There was new life among us, and as this new generation of our family was emerging and, with both my brothers having already had children, we wondered how the world's leaders could have let another war happen.

When, in May 1939 you arrived, Maureen, and then in 1941, my dear grandson, Bobby, and finally you, my sweet little Pattie, in 1944, I felt my heart would burst with love for you all. Although you were all born in wartime – as if we hadn't had enough of wars – you all offered so much hope. By that time I had been through so much, seen so much, and lost so many people I loved dearly, and at last there was something which had lightened my life.

When you were youngsters and we listened on the crackling wireless about how the war was ravaging the heart out of our homeland's streets, I used to hug you all close to me and distract you by telling you the stories of the grandfather you had never met.

But what a world you were all brought into, with air raid sirens and the threat of bombings across the city. When you were little we did the best we could to keep you all safe, and when those sirens rang out you would go with your Mum and Dad, with you, Maureen and Bobby, holding hands, and Pattie, you just a babe in arms clinging to your father's side as you all scurried along the street in a crocodile formation to the relative safety of the shelter.

Me, though, I think that by then I had become immune to war, which seems a strange thing for me to say, but it was, indeed, a strange feeling. I was working for the munitions factory, and as I automated my movements in synchronicity with the machinery, well, I suppose that gave me a lot of time to think about Jack and reflect on all we had been through together. And then when I was at home and the sirens bellowed along the street, I turned out the lights and made myself and little Penny a bed under the kitchen table. I wanted to be alone. I don't know why I didn't go with you all to the shelter; I think I was just happier here with my own thoughts. Perhaps

I had seen so much and lost so much that hiding there in a cocoon with the windows blacked out and a drink and a cigarette or two – I suppose that was all I needed – just to wait it out and leave my life in the hands of fate. I wasn't frightened, as by then death was no longer something I feared. Death had taken such beautiful, gentle people away from me, that by then I had stopped wondering why.

Time passed and there was new hope with these new generations who we hoped would learn from the mistakes of their elders. At the outbreak of the Second World War, my brother Tom had joined up as part of the Home Guard and used to bring his rifle home with him – his son Fred was just eight years old at the time and used to play 'soldiers' with Tom's army cap – luckily he wasn't allowed to play with the rifle.

As part of his wartime duties, Tom went to work as a policeman at the gates of the munitions plant and security was very tight. This was also where I was working during the war and you had to show a special card each time you entered the complex. They were making bullets for the Allies, you see. The Germans must have known what was going on there because the bombers used to come low over the building terrifying the daylights out of those of us who were inside; if we were unfortunate enough to be walking from building to building when they came over, we could see the bombs hanging underneath the planes.

There were home guard soldiers manning big guns in the parks, and when the air raid sirens rang out you could hear the automatic fire of these guns in the distance as they tried to bring down the enemy's planes.

We often used to see the Prisoners of War, as a lot of them were held near to Swanshurst Park. They used to make wooden birds which they gave to us to pass on to the local children. You'll remember those, Maureen, as you were given one of them. The wood was intricately carved, and the wings moved on a string to make it look as though the bird was flying.

The German soldiers became very good at speaking English and communication between us all was quite free by the end of the war. A couple of local ladies found themselves marrying German POWs once the war was over. Just as it was after the First World War, it was hard to comprehend who our enemy had been, when we found ourselves chatting to these men who looked just like us, and who breathed the same air.

You three were all too young to be evacuated, but like so many children from Birmingham, because he was older, Tom's son Fred was sent to the countryside for three years during the war. In 1941, Tom and his wife Floss (there was in increasing number of Florences in the family) had decided Fred should be one of those to go on the buses which were leaving for the countryside from Fred's school in Yardley Wood. Many of the children were excited, not realising they would not be living with their parents again for several years. That night they would be sleeping in strange beds in strange towns, in houses with strange people, and not all of them would be kind people either.

At the end of their journey, the children arrived at another school clutching their bags and with their little gas masks attached to them – just in case! This was where they were sorted out and chosen by whoever took a liking to them. Tom's Fred was chosen, along with another boy, to go with a sixty year old spinster named Miss Leedham. Once she had chosen the two of them she led them out of the school by their hands, one either side of her. For the three years away from their parents they lived in Miss Leedham's large house which could be seen from the whole village. Fred was one of the luckier evacuated children, and had a good time with this lady and the other boy. Tom and the rest of the family made sure they went to see him regularly, but leaving him there each time was hard for them and, no doubt, hard for him too.

After the war Tom became a park ranger for the Birmingham parks – something he did until he retired. There was a huge pond in Swanshurst Park, and one day he noticed that a little girl was in there drowning. Well, he just dived straight in there and saved her life. He became something of a local hero for a little while after that, but what his act of bravery also did was to highlight to him that he wasn't quite as fit as he thought he was. The pneumonia he had suffered from in India back in The Great War had left him quite debilitated, and he would often be quite short of breath. After that event he decided he should slow down a bit and look after himself.

In 1943, my own father, the formidable William Holmes, died. He left behind his second wife, Emma, who passed away seven years after him. She was a lovely woman, but she never really filled the gap that had been left by my own mother all those years before. I suppose it would have been impossible for her to have done so. Emma kept my father happy, however, and they loved each other dearly. They never had children of their own. I imagine that by the time they married they were both too old to think about such things, but Emma was very fond of my little brother Sam and became his mentor, guiding him and helping him until the day she died. I don't know whether Sam had been affected by the traumas of his childhood, but he lived a lonely, almost reclusive, life.

Father had maintained his ability to thrive in even the most desperate of situations, skills learnt all those years before when he had fought in the Boer War and subsequently during his time in the forces in Sitapur in India, where I was born. These skills continued until the day he died – even on his deathbed he was concerned about his wife Emma's wartime food supplies.

In 1936 my sister, Florrie, moved west and went to live in America to work as a nurse. I'll never know what happened between us. She did marry – a lovely man called Will, but he died very young – I don't know of what. He died and she went away, and that was the last I heard from her. Just after she left I found out her address from Sam and wrote to her, but there was a resistance there I shall never understand. It seems as though whatever feelings she had on mine and Jack's wedding day, well, perhaps they really were a premonition of how we were going to lose the closeness we had had when we were growing up. As far as I'm aware now, twenty years after she went away, she is still in America, but she could be anywhere in this world and I would not know for sure where she was, or what she was doing.

The lovely Mr. Curtis, the baker, died – I never knew how old he was, just that he always seemed much older than I was. It is like that when you're young – even someone who is just ten years older than you can seem as though they are much, much older. But then they seem to go on for years and you think that perhaps they must be on their 'last legs'. Then you look in the mirror at the lines around your eyes, the ones at the corners of your mouth, and at the sagging skin of your neck, all of which seem to have appeared in a matter of days, and you see that, actually, they mustn't be much older than you. It's a strange thing, ageing, it catches up with you, and the feeling you have inside that you are still in your twenties, I suppose that never really goes away, even when the mirror defies your inner perceptions of yourself.

That Mr. Curtis, he was a good, kind man, and even when you three were quite small, he still had his bakery and I used to take you along there – but you were all so young at the time that you probably wouldn't remember.

War memorials were being built in towns, cities and in the centre of small villages and hamlets all over the world which bore evidence to the loss of our war dead. Crosses or elaborate plinths with bronze soldiers posing atop them bearing the weapons of war appeared on street corners and in shopping centres.

But there were no war memorials being engraved with the names of men like Jack: men who *did* return from the war, but whose wars beat them not just physically but psychologically, too. The war had stolen their minds and their personalities – everything they were before had been left on the battlefield and been buried in the mud with their dead comrades.

So many, many people lost their lives and our family's future was changed irrevocably by the losses of George, Edwin and my dear Jack. Perhaps through my passing this story on to you, my dear grandchildren, and through others like me passing on their own stories of all that maiming and destruction of life, the remembrance of the atrocious wars will continue through the generations and serve as a torch which can be passed, baton by baton, into the future.

You are all but grown now, and I fear I shall not live to see you marry and have your own children. Please take this story and keep it safe and in your hearts. When your children are old enough, tell them all you know – never faltering from the truth. It is our responsibility to keep this flame alive.

Only then will the world never see the likes of what happened back then ever again.

Chapter 10

November 1957 – Grace

Wearing their best Sunday clothes and all dressed in black, they stood beside the freshly-dug grave of their grandmother. Maureen held tightly to her father's arm, Florence was gripping her husband's other arm, her fingernails blanching his skin. Fearful her mother would collapse, Pattie, still just a child of twelve years of age, and hardly knowing much of death, held tightly to her mother's other hand. Bobby stood beside them all, with his ashen face fixed in an expression of despair, staring into the open grave.

Each of them was unable to comprehend the sudden loss of their dear grandmother. She had been coughing for a while, and had never quite managed to shake off the virus she had caught earlier on in the autumn – that was all they had thought was wrong with her, just a virus she was having difficulty getting rid of. The autopsy confirmed she had been suffering with pneumonia – the smoking she had begun back in the tumultuous years of The Great War had finally caught up with her.

The minister finished his sermon, ending with the Lord's Prayer. After dropping roses and sprinkling handfuls of soil into the grave, Grace's brother Tom and his wife Floss, Bill and his wife Hilda, and Grace's youngest brother Sam, followed the rest of their family towards the row of funeral cars. Others had come to congregate around the grave and they would follow the family when they headed back to the house. "A good turnout," Maureen overheard someone say.

*

Just less than a week before, Grace hadn't turned up at Florence and Robert's house when she was meant to. On Tuesdays she was always at Florence's by 10.30am – it was something she had always done ever since she had become old enough to draw her pension. When they couldn't contact her by telephone, worried that her mother was unwell, Florence suggested to Robert that they should go and find out whether she was all right. They reached for their coats and headed towards the front door.

By coincidence, Maureen had turned up at the same time with her new fiancé, Tony, intending to show Grace and her parents her engagement ring and, when Robert opened the door, Maureen burst into the room, flushed with excitement and called out 'Gran, Gran, I have a surprise for you.' Immediately seeing the look on her mother and father's faces, she knew something was wrong.

Now in a panic, the four of them piled into Robert's car and headed to Grace's house. As soon as they arrived they saw little Tommy up at the front window making a racket. There was a sense of urgency about the way in which he was barking. When he saw them through the window, he dashed into the hall, and Robert could see him through the frosted glass. Robert knocked at the door. Nothing – except the increasingly desperate barking from the other side of the door.

He knocked again.

Nothing.

He and Tony walked to the front window and strained their eyes to see through the net curtain. Tommy reappeared, and as the little dog jumped back up onto the windowsill the curtain moved, allowing Tony and Robert a momentary glimpse of the room inside – Grace was lying on the floor.

'Oh, dear God,' Robert called out, and raced back to the front door. He tried to force it open, but to no avail. And then he had an idea.

'The entry.'

Between the terraced houses was an entry which took you along a cobbled pathway through to the back gardens – Grace may have left the back kitchen door unlocked – especially if she had taken ill sometime the previous evening, before she had had a chance to lock the doors. She had. They all raced through the kitchen, on through the sitting room, and into the front room. Tommy raced around their heels; he was so pleased someone had come at last.

Grace had still been conscious, but only just. Without delay, Robert called an ambulance, and within minutes Grace was being transferred onto a stretcher. Florence and Robert very quickly made the decision that Tony and Maureen should go in the ambulance with Grace, and they would follow on in their car once they had taken Tommy back to their house.

Holding onto her grandmother's hand, and only subconsciously aware of the blaring sound of the siren which was telling passers-by that someone was in need of help, Maureen felt that Grace's life was slipping away. The culmination of her life was as a much-loved mother and grandmother – whatever she had been before, the places she had travelled and the lives she had touched – in the end her greatest joy had been spending time with those she loved.

Gathering Tommy and his lead, Robert and Florence bundled the little dog in the car and took him home with them. Giving him a drink of water and some dog food they had grabbed from Grace's kitchen, they patted him on the head and left him to his own devices – perhaps to wonder at all the commotion. Florence was distraught by this time. Having lost her father in such tragic circumstances when she was so young, her mother had been the one constant presence in her life until that point; the one individual on whom she had relied since the day she was born, and now suddenly she would no longer be there. They arrived at the hospital just in time for her to say farewell to her mother for the last time.

*

After her funeral, and once all the relatives had gone home, Florence, Robert, Maureen and her fiancé Tony, along with Bobby and Pattie, sat huddled around the fire reminiscing about Grace and the life she had led.

Bob left the room and came back with his grandmother's book, the one she had made and given to them just a year before. On the first page of the book Grace had carefully attached two sepia photographs – one of her and one of Jack, both of them taken on their wedding day, that freezing cold Christmas Eve of 1912, so very long ago when they had walked into the church on The Green, in Kings Norton. Grace had her centrally-parted dark brown hair swept back from her face and was wearing her high-necked dress with a lace-trimmed bodice and decorative buttons up the front. Her smile was one of anticipated happiness and joy for the life they would have together. Jack was sporting his generous moustache, neatly combed hair and Sunday-best clothes, a guarded smile touching his lips.

They had been together in life and, however little time

they had spent together, he had always been a part of her, and they were now together for eternity in the grave on the hill.

The Author's Memories and Research

What inspires us to write the things we do? Is it morbid to have a desire to respond to an echo from the past, and constantly revive events that were experienced by those whom we know only by name? Is there sense in the curiosity we have in people's lives when we have our own lives to live?

Jack and Grace Cogbill and, by a twist of fate, George and Agnes Cogbill, were all my great-grandparents. Jack and Grace were on my mother's side of the family, and George and Agnes on my father's side.

When I chanced upon this story back in 2010 or 2011, it became somewhat of an obsession for me to find out more about their lives. I had to do everything I could to make sure that in some way their story was recorded. I have spoken to relatives who knew, and loved, Grace, and it very quickly became obvious to me that she had to be the central focus of the story – she and her husband Jack. Her life was not an easy one, but she was strong, and she became everyone's emotional support through all that happened.

I wish I had met her and been able to sit down with her and have a chat, but she died eight years before I was born... so all I know about the First World War I have had to piece together little by little and wrap around Jack and Grace's tale.

The Great War is a subject I heard about briefly (far too briefly) during senior history classes when at school in Kings Heath in Birmingham. I existed in my own world, and spent far too much time staring out of the window trying to capture glimpses of wild birds roosting on the branches of the jungle of trees, which each autumn would cast their golden leaves into the school pond, rather than thinking about the importance of my classes. Eventually, the subjects I was to take to examination level became influenced by how much they would help me to work with animals or, I'm ashamed to say, how much I liked the teacher. When the time came and I'd chosen the ones I needed to become a veterinary nurse, my final choice was whether to take history or geography and, as I have regretted many times over the years, I chose the latter.

So, my memories of the short time I spent learning history are few, but the lessons that continue to reside in my mind are those in which women were the central characters: Lady Jane Grey and her very short reign as Queen of England; the extensive reign of Queen Victoria; the sufferance of the Suffragettes; the mediaeval 'witches' who ended their lives on the 'ducking chair' or by being burned at the stake (tales which continue to haunt me to this day), and the incarceration of Anne Frank and her family as they hid in Amsterdam from the Nazis in the Second World War. We listened in class to her story on a cassette tape, and it fascinated me; but I had no other interest in war and conflict, only in preventing it – even at such a young age I considered myself to be a pacifist. I was (and continue to be) idealistic, and already fighting my own wars against factory farms, vivisection, seal clubbing and 'banning the bomb', attending as many demonstrations as I could to feel as though I was doing something to protect our fragile earth.

Meanwhile, at school the story of The Great War was certainly mentioned, but somehow I allowed whatever I heard to wash over me, listening but not absorbing. At that time I didn't know the enormity of just how important this event was in our history and, in particular, its relevance to my own family. It was many years later that my interest in it began, not with my horror at the atrocities of what had happened in the trenches, but with Grace.

Throughout my childhood she had been there, like some legend hovering over us in the background bestowing all her love on us like an angel. There was no doubt that she was adored by the older generations of the family, but to me, back then, she was simply a faded black and white – almost sepia, image that tumbled out of an old white handbag each time we three remaining generations had an opportunity to sit and reminisce about the 'olden days'.

My grandmother, Grace's daughter Florence, kept this tattered, white handbag stuffed with photographs of those who were long gone. As the only granddaughter, and with the boys being older and preferring to spend their time playing at the back of the terraced houses, whose back gardens opened onto the banks of the River Rea, my mother, aunt, grandmother, and I used to gather around the fireplace and open the bag, each time releasing the musty scent of the family's history. Huddled together, we'd go through the photographs one by one, and they'd tell me all about how these people in their strange clothes related to me.

"Oh, that would have been your great, great uncle... oh, and just look at that – that's your grandfather's cousin." These comments would invariably be accompanied by puzzled looks as they furrowed their brows and raised their gazes to the ceiling while they tried to work out who was who, and how the network of cousins twice or three times removed pieced together. But the images that brought tears to their eyes, or gave them a faraway look whenever they gripped hold of their corners, were those monochrome photographs of Grace, and her husband Jack. They must have told me the stories of these people's lives time and time again, and I wish now that I had listened to them more intently; that I had allowed my immature mind to absorb them; to concentrate hard and focus on what they were telling me, because time passes, and the ones who really know what happened pass on, and their tales are lost forever. It's only when you're older yourself and you realise the fragility of life, that you want to know more, but by then the information has become so much more difficult to find, and memories have become frayed.

It has taken me a long time to finally get around to writing what remnants of their story remain. Everything in this book I've had to discover through reading multiple texts, watching documentaries, reading web pages, and having hundreds of conversations. I have then had to articulate it in such a way that it makes sense. I have dabbled with this for several years, and it is a journey which I have had a great urge to bring to fruition. More than anything, however, I hope that this is a tribute to those who gave their lives. All along I have wanted to do them and their story justice and, simultaneously, try to reflect what happened in their war with what happened to others who lived (and died) through that period.

Grace never remarried and did not live long enough to see any of her great-grandchildren. She had lived through two world wars and had to endure Jack's untimely death and that of two of his brothers, her sister, mother and her tiny baby girl, Adeline. I suppose the effects of nicotine and alcohol helped to numb the memories of what she had been through and, perhaps in some way, that was her way of coping with the effects of the life she had been dealt and the loss of so many around her.

Grace has fascinated me ever since I rediscovered her photograph a few years ago. She made me want to know more about her and the life she led. This rediscovery of her picture coincided with me having conversations with family members about Jack and his war and the story of his post-war problems began to piece together little by little. Looking at the fusion of these two very different families – the Cogbills and the Holmes', and then finding out shortly afterwards that Jack had lost two of his brothers to the Great War led me down tangents which resulted in all sorts of side-issues such as boy soldiers, mosquitoes and tuberculosis. Each avenue I went down the story became more and more interesting. I could have made this story longer by creating a vast array of fictional events, but in the end I decided to remain as true to the story as I could – and so it has become more or less as it has been told to me by members of the family, and much of it has been corroborated by documents I have uncovered in my research.

In 1995, perhaps with a sense of his own mortality, and with a need to express the importance of family history being passed down through the generations, Fred Holmes, Grace's nephew and her brother Tom's son, who long ago was one of our disparate family who emigrated to America, gathered together as many family photographs as he could find and wrote everything he knew about each person. In his album he talks fondly of Grace, and I feel a sense of duty, but also pride, to include some of what he says about her here:

"... My mother and father used to take me to see her. Grace was a pleasant woman. She always had a smile on her face and, as I remember her, she only had a couple or more big teeth. I don't think she had any false teeth. One thing she would always get was her two bottles of beer, family ale, that's what it may have been. You would take an empty bottle to the outdoor and have it filled up."

He goes on to explain about an outdoor being an off-licence, and then, "You would not drink beer in there, but you could smell the strong smell of it when you walked in. Grace got her beer supply from the outdoor on the corner just across the road, and so they all sat around talking and having a drink whenever we used to visit her. I don't know if she ever smoked, her teeth were stained – I can see her smiling now. I used to go into the back yard and play. It was only a small garden, with not much to look at, and not much outlook. An entry used to run along the side of the house, and in the garden the high wall used to separate the entry, and another high wall at the end of the garden blocked the view. The wall must have been the back of a stable, as I remember a few times a man bringing a horse up the entry after a day's work; you could hear the horse clomping up the entry. It was a floor made of blue bricks. I didn't ever know what the horses were used for. In those days they pulled all sorts of carts – they were the big heavy horses, and you don't see many of them today."

Fred continues with another of his vivid memories: "I remember one day we went to Grace's home. I loved to go there and that evening it started to rain with thunder and lightning. When it was time to go home, I did not go as the weather was too bad, so my mother and father left me there and I slept in the little back room, listening to the storm."

His final entry about her is when he talks about going to her house when he was in his twenties. "One time my father and I went to her house and Dad spoke to whoever was there, I didn't know them, and we only stayed a few moments – Grace had passed away."

Fred was also able to enlighten me as to the whereabouts of Grace's sister, Florrie, and how she had lived her life once she reached America. Grace never knew for sure what had happened to her – Florrie actually outlived all of her generation (and many of the next), eventually dying in January 1986 at the age of ninety-four. Like Grace, she was born in India, lived in Africa, Ireland, and the UK, but then spent over fifty years in Florida – America very much became her home. She had, indeed, as Grace thought, become a nurse, and she spent her whole career there working in nursing, being instrumental in bringing about the licensing of Practical Nurses.

My Aunt Pat has strong memories of Grace – she has stayed in her thoughts all these decades since her death, and even now, like my late mum did, she still regularly talks about 'Gran'. There are some people who touch your life who, I imagine, you will never forget, and who remain a part of you until the day you die.

As Grace's eldest grandchild, my mum, Maureen, vividly remembered those times during World War Two when she and the rest of the family had to rush to the air raid shelter when the sirens rang out through Birmingham, but how Grace had insisted on *not* going with them. She had worried about her grandmother, but what could she do? Their mother,

Florence, was often quite sick; she was beautiful, but her constitution was quite weak. On many occasions Grace stepped in and went over to look after the children.

One of Aunt Pat's strongest memories about Grace is the toast which she always burned. Her cooking was unpredictable, but they all got used to putting up with spoiled food, because the thrill of her company and the enjoyment and love they gleaned from days with their grandmother, far outweighed any potential adverse effects on their digestive systems.

When she was young, Aunt Pat and her friend used to go and do Grace's cleaning in exchange for a portion of fish and chips. On one of these occasions, Grace noticed they hadn't polished the piano's legs, so they had to wait and get their supper once they had completed their task.

When she babysat, Grace would take her grandchildren to the wood yard to gather wood to make things. With help from my grandfather, Robert, they would all make great items such as trolleys, dolls' cots and bookcases. Aunt Pat's one regret is that, because she was only thirteen when Grace died, she felt she didn't ask enough about Grace's own childhood in India, Africa and Ireland. For Mum, too, this was something she regretted.

Mum also had strong memories of the day Grace died – she had been so excited to show Grace the engagement ring that day in November 1957, and her world had fallen apart when she and my dad had instead ended up accompanying Grace to the hospital in the ambulance.

Through being able to find all this out about Grace, and knowing how much she meant to Mum, my Aunt Pat, my late Uncle Bob, and Grace's brother Tom Holmes' son, Fred, I have been able to discover a lot about her from people who loved her. I feel that in writing this I had to use Grace as one of the central focuses of my story. In gratitude to her and to all they went through, all that I have written and recorded here has really been for them – Jack and Grace.

Jack and Grace lie together in a family grave in a huge cemetery in the West Midlands. If you walk along the paths that divide the old graves from the new, and the Catholics from the Protestants, and head towards the top of the hill, where many of the other graves are now untended because the relatives of those who lie there have long since passed, then you would almost walk on by. But this is where Jack and Grace have lain together since she died in 1957. Some years ago, when people realised the value of old rope-top kerbstones for selling to those who were blessed with large, well-stocked gardens, the stones that surrounded their grave 'disappeared', leaving the grave completely unmarked. Out of the corner of your eye as you walk along the paths, you might see a small rose bush that was regularly tended until his death by my Uncle Bob, who went to the cemetery on special days to visit the graves of his parents and grandparents. It being a family grave, he also now rests there.

There is now a stone which marks the grave of this ordinary couple who began their lives together in a time of optimism and joy, only to have their world shattered by a war on foreign shores. The engraving on the stone honours Jack's time in Salonica during this 'war to end all wars', and anyone who walks on by will, at last, know something of the story of this soldier and the woman he loved.

I began my conclusion to this book by talking about the women in history who had wedged themselves in my mind from my limited number of history lessons. What makes a person so great? Birthright? Fortune? Fame? Or is it the wholeness of a person's character and their capacity to cope with the worst that life has to throw at them, while bringing joy to others around them? If that is so, then Grace was such a person.

Once the First World War had ended, back home food staples had started to be rationed and families found out about the deaths of their loved ones often with no knowledge of where their bodies lay. For many families there was never any sense of 'closure'. The effects of bereavement in war became evident and more widespread than they had ever been before, and as men gradually returned from the trenches to 'Civvy Street', they had to integrate back into their families among people who now appeared as strangers; people who had little concept of what they had endured, man against man, so far away from their homes and loved ones. Children who had never known their fathers had to get used to the presence of a 'stranger' in their home – a stranger often with periods of unexplained silence; times when their mental isolation was preferable to voicing their memories. Soldiers like Jack.

The health of the men suffered, not necessarily through injury, and therefore not visibly, but psychologically there was a huge remnant of the war evident. Jack, who survived his war in Greece, returned to a world in which he no longer felt he belonged. He could never fully articulate the horrors he had seen, and Grace was only able to sympathise, but never truly comprehend what he had been through.

When Jack died eight years after the war came to its conclusion, Grace was left to attempt to make a life for herself and her daughter. Her life had shifted focus from that of someone who was trying to cope with the ghosts of her husband's past, to that of a mother and, subsequently, a grandmother.

Grace never remarried – this seems to be fairly typical of many women from that generation, they had seen and heard so much that perhaps they preferred it to be that way. There was a dearth of men of their generation due to losses of life during the war, and the women those soldiers left behind, women like Grace, often seemed to be content to simply have their families around them, spending their lives as widows with the memories of what life was like before the war had devastated their world.

Edwin and George are remembered through inscriptions of their names on memorials in Europe. Edwin's body was never recovered and is somewhere in France, lying alongside those of other troops who died in the Battle of the Somme. His name is listed on the Thiepval Memorial, next to the village of Thiepval in northern France and, according to the Commonwealth War Graves Commission, this memorial "bears the names of more than seventy-two thousand officers and men of the United Kingdom and South African forces who died in the Somme sector before 20 March 1918 and who have no known grave. Over 90% of those commemorated died between July and November 1916. The memorial also serves as an Anglo-French Battle Memorial in recognition of the joint nature of the 1916 offensive."

I have no photographs of Edwin, and have scanned the faces of many images of troops from his regiment, but the searching has been to no avail. I imagine I see him, but there's doubt in my mind as I look across the seas and seas of faces, and realise that they all look so similar to one another – the same haircuts and the same grey, weary faces. In Fairclough's book of 1933, there's a photograph which shows the troops marching through the streets of Birmingham in March 1915, and as I sit here a century in the future, it's difficult to imagine the thoughts of the men in the line; of what they thought they would be eventually marching into. The war had been underway for over seven months, so they knew that it was for real and that it was showing no signs of being resolved any day soon. They would have known others who had died, but does some primeval urge take over and block out the threat to yourself in favour of the duty that you are undertaking to protect your country and those back home?

Edwin would have been on that march, I am sure of it, and I've looked blindly among those faces trying to recognise some family resemblance in these young men, attempting to find the face of this seventeen-year old who was never going to marry, never have children, never see his family, and never see the shores of his homeland again.

The truth is, however, that any one of them could be Edwin.

George's name is listed on the Ploegsteert memorial, West Vlaanderen, in memory of the 11,447 British men who died fighting between the River Douve and the French towns of Estaires and Furnes (in Nord, Northern France). None of the men who have their names listed on the memorial has a known burial site. This memorial was established following the ground been given by Belgium to the United Kingdom in honour of the sacrifices made by so many people of the British Empire. As described by the Commonwealth Graves Commission, 'Most were killed in the course of the day-to-day trench warfare which characterised this part of the line, or in small-scale set engagements, usually carried out in support of the major attacks taking place elsewhere'.

*

Back in Birmingham, Saint Nicolas Church, where George and Agnes married in 1906, and Jack and Grace in 1912, is a Church of England church which underwent some major restoration during the years from 1860–1872, including the addition of a vicarage nearby. Beside the church, around the triangle that is 'The Green', there lies a series of magnificent buildings which date back as far as the 1200s. Now collectively known as Saint Nicolas Place, the Church, the Saracen's Head and The Old Grammar School were lucky enough to be part of a BBC television restoration in 2004.

The Saracen's Head is currently the Parish Office, but in times gone by it was an old wool merchant's house, which was originally owned by the Rotsey family, themselves dealers in wool. By the time of Jack and Grace's wedding in 1912, it had long since become a public house. When standing in front of these examples of Mediaeval architecture, you can't help but think of those who must have stood on that piece of ground in all the years since these buildings were erected, and marvel at the effort that must have gone into constructing them at a time when modern tools and machinery were not available.

It instils a great feeling of pride that somewhere in this area's history, there was a time when my own ancestors walked those streets, drank beer in that inn, and worshipped in that church. Walking in their footsteps and imagining their feelings as they went about their business a hundred years ago, I wonder from this vantage point in the future whether they anticipated the onset of the war that was to change all their lives forever.

Just a short glance away from this church on The Green in Kings Norton, in years gone by there was a cinema. We used to go there every Sunday in the 1970s.

Lazing outside on the steps in the sunshine, or sheltering from the rain under the overhang of the building, we used to wait in great anticipation and immense eagerness outside that cinema, or 'the pictures' as we used to call it, for the time we'd be allowed inside to settle ourselves ready for the double-bill of films we were about to watch. Like so many traditional cinemas, now that the multiplexes have dominated the world of film viewing, this cinema of my past was closed in 1983. It was left boarded up and became derelict for a while, before eventually being demolished and the site used for housing.

But it was not the cinema of my youth that took me back to The Green a couple of years ago, but the church itself, for I wanted to see the plaques showing the names of those who fell in the two World Wars. I was overwhelmed when there, for all passers-by to read, if they had the time to stop for a few moments, among the names of others who fell, was George's name. How many times I must have walked past the church and not known, not stood with a sense of pride and absorbed the enormity of the loss of this man. Every one of those men on that list deserves to be remembered for the part they had in the war. All over the country there are plaques such as this one, and as we pass by we can perhaps do their memory a little justice by taking a few moments to stop and whisper some of their names. Whether we are related to them or not, it shouldn't matter – they gave their lives not because they wanted to, but because it was expected of them, and that was how things turned out for them – in the end, it was the luck of the draw.

When we were young, and as we stood chatting and waiting for the massive cinema doors to open, I don't recall my brother and me ever being told about the gate to the church that was no more than a hundred yards from where we stood, and its importance to our family. I can only assume that they didn't know that George's name was commemorated there and, if they did, then perhaps they thought that our excitement about the latest Disney film would only be marred by talk of war and of people we would never know. "Lady and the Tramp" or "Snow White and the Seven Dwarves" were far more appropriate for Sunday afternoon escapism than dwelling on talk of death and destruction. A generation had separated our parents from those who had experienced the First World War. In the interim, as children themselves, there had been another World War, which had given them their own memories of a world in conflict. Time had passed, and in their adulthood our parents were of a generation who had experienced peace, social advancement, and great industrial progress in the Western world.

I am sure our family's loss of two of its sons as a direct consequence of the war is not unusual – and, if we include Jack, which I feel we should, then there were three brothers who died (or who had their lives ruined) because of the conflict. It was very difficult for men to avoid going to fight, and there were so many lives lost that a lot of families were all but destroyed by the war. One of the largest familial losses of life through fighting in the UK was a family from Lincolnshire – the Beechey family, who lost five of its sons. There are many other cases of two, three or four sons having been lost.

To lose any son is colossal – to a mother who has only one son, the loss of him is devastating, and there were many, many mothers and fathers who lost their whole male line to the war. The war wrought absolute destruction to the lives of so many families. The truth is, that one person dying changes the course of that family's future. The loss of George, Edwin, and then Jack, for instance, has been felt through the last century by subsequent generations. One death changes everything.

There are no specific memorials for soldiers like Jack: soldiers who fought and then returned, only to live out their days in misery until one day their flame was extinguished and their stories left untold, in Jack's case for nearly a century. Men returned from the war and most didn't utter a word of what they had seen until many years later, keeping all that they had experienced nestled deep inside them like an unexploded time bomb, until they finally let it all come out and told their story. Some never told what they had experienced – even secretly to their loved ones – they kept it all locked inside them and took it with them to the grave; or the horrors they saw were relived each time they tossed and turned in their beds, when they screamed out for their lost comrades.

Much of Jack and Grace's story is set in Stirchley, where they lived, and Bournville, where Jack worked prior to the war. Bournville village is encapsulated as a part of the City of Birmingham, and perhaps is now very far removed from being anything like a typical village in the true sense of the word but, as you wander along the wide streets and gaze in awe at the colourful array of flowers that the residents have so carefully tended, or sit under the trees on the village green on a warm summer's day, you get the sense that this is a place with a solid history; a place for which time has dedicated its all. There are many other places like this in Birmingham – places where, although people are rushing around going about their business, if you take the time to stop and stare, you will see the beauty of the gardens, the buildings, the tree-lined streets, and the large, open spaces.

I now have my great-grandfather Jack's medals, and it gives me great comfort to have them here with me after all these years. My uncle Bob took care of the medals for fifty-six years after Grace passed away, and I inherited them when he died in 2013. They mean so much to me. Jack's name is engraved along their edge, something which was done to all medals for their recipients. The medals are still in the packaging in which they would have been posted to Jack, and I keep them safely with his and Grace's photographs and other items that belonged to them.

I don't know the whereabouts of Edwin or George's service medals, and unless they lie at the bottom of a Birmingham landfill site, then they must be somewhere, someone must have them, even if they don't realise they have them. I only hope that, wherever they are, they are appreciated for their worth, and for the lives these two men lived and their unfortunate premature deaths.

I found Grace's engagement ring among some boxes that Mum gave me to have a look through. I went through each box, uncovering in each one long-forgotten pieces of the past – an amber teardrop-shaped necklace that my late father had given to Mum in the 1960s; a small jewellery box an old friend had given her; and a pearl necklace which had belonged to my grandmother.

When I found the ring I immediately recognised it, for it had temporarily adorned my hand many years before when I had discovered it while I was helping Mum to sort her wardrobe out. At the time she had told me that one day it would be mine, and I had never forgotten her saying that to me. And here it was again, within minutes secured to the ring finger of my right hand. Missing its original diamond, it was not worth much in monetary terms, and even fixed with another gem in place as it is now, it is not worth much more, but that's not what it's about is it? This ring is over a century old and it originated from a time when there was hope – a time before the two world wars shed their blood across so many countries, and all those lives were forsaken. It represents a piece of history.

The ring is the one that Jack gave her; the ring that bound them to one another. It had been a declaration of their promise to each other of the years to come – the years they would spend together. It fits me perfectly and I have extremely small fingers. I feel as though it has been waiting for me all these years – for a time when I would appreciate its worth and cherish this contact with the people who I knew previously only by name, but who I now feel I know as though they are friends who have been with me for my whole life.

There have been conflicts since and there were many before, and each death is bloody, unnecessary and an atrocity. We need to treat each individual who loses or lost their life as someone special; someone who lived and loved and gave a massive contribution to the lives that we now have.

We should never, ever forget that.

And those who have been here before are there

Not fearful, nor lost

Just anticipating

Waiting

(Clare Cogbill, 2014)

Bibliography

The following books and web pages have been invaluable in enabling me to pull together the pieces of this story – I am in deep gratitude to the authors of these works:

Ancestry, multiple pages, links and searches, ancestry.co.uk

Arthur, Max, *Lost Voices of the Edwardians*, 2nd Edition (2007), Transcript of the voice of Florence Hannah warn, Harper Perennial, UK

BBC History, *Battle of the Somme* (1st July – 13th November 1916), (Online, accessed 22nd October 2013)http://www.bbc.co.uk/history/worldwars/wwone/battle_somme.shtml

BBC Inside Out, *Shell Shock*, 3rd March 2004, updated 2005, (online, accessed 22nd October 2013), http://www.bbc.co.uk/insideout/extra/series-1/shell_shocked.shtml

Barham, P, *Forgotten Lunatics of the Great War*, (2007), Yale University Press, London, UK

Barry, J.M., *The Great Influenza: The Story of the Deadliest Pandemic in History*, (2009 reprint), Penguin Books, UK

Birmingham Cemeteries, (Online, accessed 20th April 2012)www.brumagem.co.uk/Cemeteries_2_Birmingham.shtm

Birmingham City Council, Online, accessed 10th April 2012), www.birmingham.gov.uk/thegreen

Bridger, G, *The Great War Handbook, A Guide for Family Historians and Students* (2009), Pen and Sword Books Limited, UK

Cadbury Limited booklet, *The Story of Cadbury Limited*, Cadbury Limited, Bournville, Birmingham B30 2LU, UK

Cadbury Limited booklet, *The History of Cadbury*, Cadbury Limited, Bournville, Birmingham B30 2LU

Carter, T. (Lieut-Colonel), *1914-1918*, invisionzone.com (posted May 2008) (Online)

Carter, T, *Birmingham Pals: 14th, 15th & 16th (Service) Battalions of the Royal Warwickshire Regiment: a History of the Three City Battalions Raised in Birmingham in World War One*, (1997), Pen and Sword Books Limited, Yorkshire, UK

Census, *Longevity of Health Characteristics*, (Online) (accessed 25th October 2013)

Chin, C., *The Cadbury Story* (2000), Brewin Books, Warwickshire, UK

Collinson-Owen, H., *Salonica and After*, (no date – pre–1923), Reprint (2013) Shelf2life Programme, KU Libraries, Kansas/ Lightning Source UK Limited, Milton Keynes, UK

CWGC, Commonwealth War Graves Commission cemetery details, (Online – accessed 27th April 2012) www.cwgc.org/findacemetery

Demidowicz, G & Price, S., *King's Norton – A History*, (2009), Phillimore & Co. Limited, Chichester, West Sussex, England

Doyle, Peter, *First World War Britain 1914–1919*, (2012), Shire Living Histories – 'How we worked, how we played, how we lived' series, UK

Genes Reunited, multiple pages, links and searches,

genesreunited.co.uk

Holmes, Frederick, *The Story of the Holmes Family*, (1994/5), unpublished works, Florida, USA

Lethbridge, J.P., *Birmingham in the First World War*, Newgate Press, (1993)

Martin, Jack, *Sapper Martin: The Secret Great War Diary of Jack Martin*, Edited and Introduced by Richard van Emden (2009), Bloomsbury Publishing, London

National Records and Archives, (Online – accessed 16th April) 2012www.archives.gov/exhibits/influenza-epidemic/

Price, G. Ward, *The Story of the Salonica Army* (1918), Edward J. Clode, Forgotten Books reprint, Amazon, UK

Science Museum, *Diseases and Epidemics*, (Online, accessed 25th October 2012) www.sciencemuseum.org.uk

Simpkin, John, *Order of the White Feather*, (1997), (Online, accessed 19th October 2013) http://www.spartacus.schoolnet.co.uk/FWWfeather

Strachan, Hew, *The Oxford Illustrated History of the First World War*, (1998), Oxford University Press, UK

Tilden, J.H. (Dr.), *Diseases of Women and Childbirth*, (1912), Kessinger Publishing Company (reprints), Montana, USA

Upton, Chris, Birmingham Post (Online – accessed 10th April 2012), www.birminghampost.net/life-leisure-birmingham-guide/postfeatures/2009/01/09/

Van Emden, Richard, *Boy Soldiers of the Great War, Their Own Stories for the First Time*, (2005), Headline Book Publishing, part of HodderHeadline, London

Walsh, Michael, *Brothers in War*, (2007), first published in 2006 by Ebury Press (Random House), United Kingdom

Worcestershire Regiment, *Shot at Dawn*, no author, (Online, accessed April 5th 2014), www.worcestershireregiment.com

World Health Organisation, *Measles Fact Sheet* no. 286, February 2013, (Online – accessed October 22nd 2013)http://www.who.int/mediacentre/factsheets/fs 286/en/

Other books by Clare Cogbill

A Dog Like Ralph

(for anyone who has ever loved a rescue dog)

The true story of Ralph, a rescue dog with a difficult past who loves other dogs, is frightened of people and cars and mesmerized by cats, rabbits and 'Santa Please Stop Here' signs. Clare, his new owner, tells with equal amounts of humour and sadness about the challenges and joys of having him as a companion.

His story is partly told through his eyes and describes how what he may have experienced before has affected how he interacts with those in his new 'forever' home. When Ralph's compatriots, Peggy and Luella, enter his life, it becomes clear that they have their own 'version of events' to add to the story!

Clare also writes about the pitfalls of a society that has resulted in Ralph being the way he is, and of how small changes could transform the plight of abandoned dogs.

This book is a tribute to the rescue dog!

Lilac Haze: Love, loss and hope

You don't remember your childhood in detail, so your memories thirty or forty years on have become hazy; times you had back then are painted in colours that have become distorted, and you find yourself recalling conversations you have created in your head.

Through living in the false world of remembering, you can deal with the past in such a way that the things that happened, they appear to matter less.

This is a love story.

In the end, anyway, that's what it will be.

A love story gives you hope: whatever you have lost; whatever you have to gain. For me, as someone on daily kidney dialysis, when an offer of a kidney came along which I couldn't possibly refuse, there was everything to gain.

But the past has a way of interfering with what seems as though it is the right path... and how do you ever in this life repay a debt so huge?

This is a true story of love, loss, grief and what can happen when you dare to hope.

If you have five minutes, please get in touch and let me know what you think of my books either on Facebook, or through my web page:

clarecogbill.com

*

I'd love to hear from you

32737060R00133

Made in the USA
Charleston, SC
24 August 2014